ALIVE IN THE SPIRIT

Also by Fr Ken Barker:

Young Men Rise Up
Amazing Love
His Name is Mercy
Becoming Fire
A Light for My Path: Scripture Prayer Journal
A Radical Way of Love

ALIVE IN THE SPIRIT

Fr Ken Barker

Modotti Press
"Where religion does matter"

Published in 2013 by Connor Court Publishing Pty Ltd

Copyright © Fr Ken Barker MGL 2013

ALL RIGHTS RESERVED. This book contains material protected under International and Federal Copyright Laws and Treaties. Any unauthorised reprint or use of this material is prohibited. No part of this book may be reproduced or transmitted in any form or by any means, electronic or mechanical, including photocopying, recording, or by any information storage and retrieval system without express written permission from the publisher.

Nihil Obstat
Rev Warrick G. Tonkin BA, DipEd, BTh, MEd.
Imprimatur
Msgr John Woods BTh, JCL.
Diocesan Administrator, Archdiocese of Canberra and Goulburn.

Modotti Press (An imprint of Connor Court Publishing).
PO Box 1
Ballan VIC 3342
sales@connorcourt.com
www.connorcourt.com

ISBN: 9781922168504 (pbk.)

Cover design by Adam Domingo MGL

Printed in Australia

CONTENTS

FOREWORD... vii

INTRODUCTION.. ix

1 A NEW PENTECOST.. 1

2 RENEWAL OF BAPTISM.. 15

3 FIRE OF LOVE... 23

4 LIGHT OF TRUTH.. 35

5 PURIFYING FIRE... 47

6 POWER TO CHANGE... 59

7 ENDOWED WITH CHARISMS................................... 75

8 COMFORTS THE AFFLICTED................................... 87

9 DELIVERANCE FROM EVIL...................................... 103

10 PRAYER IN THE SPIRIT.. 119

11 COMMUNION IN THE SPIRIT................................... 133

12 FIRE TO EVANGELIZE.. 143

13 GUIDED BY THE SPIRIT... 167

14 SPOUSE OF THE SPIRIT... 181

15 LAND OF THE SPIRIT... 187

ENDNOTES... 191

FOREWORD

Since its unexpected appearance immediately after the Second Vatican Council, the Charismatic Renewal has in one way or another entered into the life of the Catholic Church at every level; and many of the newer communities which are bringing such energy to the Church have come from within this Renewal.

In fact, charismatic spirituality has been part of the Church's life since New Testament times. Sometimes it has gone underground; at other times it has bubbled anew to the surface; and that is what has been happening in the Church for the last forty or fifty years. The Holy Spirit has been stirring among us in new ways which have enlivened not only individual Catholics but the whole Church.

In his latest book, Fr Ken Barker explains what God has been doing in breathing fresh life into the Church through the Charismatic Renewal. At times, the Church can look like a corpse; and that would be true were it not for the gift of the Holy Spirit. But because God chooses to breathe the Holy Spirit into the Church, we can speak of the Church not as a corpse but as the Body of Christ, radiant with the life that is bigger than death, the life of Easter.

Fr Ken also points out that the faith of many individual Catholics has been brought to life through the gift of the Holy Spirit. In their lives, Jesus has become not a pallid role-model who lived long ago, but a living presence and power here and now. They have experienced the love of God in a very personal and overwhelming way. The words of Scripture have come alive for them, as have the teachings of the Church, however counter-cultural they may be.

In these pages, Fr Ken weaves together Scripture, tradition and stories both autobiographical and biographical. It is a style we have seen in his earlier writings, but never more effectively than here. What he has produced is a work both old and new, both personal and ecclesial, both local and universal, both contemplative and charismatic.

This is a charismatic moment in the life of the Church where we need to ask above all, "What are the gifts which God has given?" and, "How might they be allowed to flourish for the building up of the Body of Christ for the sake of mission?" In this book, Fr Ken helps us to understand more deeply what it means to speak of this as a charismatic moment and how we might answer those questions.

He also helps us to understand more deeply how we might become a more missionary Church, and that is surely what the Spirit is saying to us at this time. However much we may be under pressure, we must head into new territory, stronger than ever in faith; and only the Holy Spirit can empower us to do that. On that point, Fr Ken leaves no doubt: the Holy Spirit is the prime mover of anything that merits the name "new evangelization".

Archbishop Mark Coleridge (Archbishop of Brisbane)

INTRODUCTION

In every age when the Church has been in crisis there has been a new surge of spiritual energy generated by a new movement of the Holy Spirit. This is true of our times. The impact of secularization, the loss of a sense of God in the minds of our contemporaries, has undoubtedly weakened the Church. The faith of many Catholics is shallow and incapable of withstanding the prevailing cultural indifference to Christianity. Increasingly we experience even blatant opposition to Christianity. Science and technology reign in the minds of many as the only way to establish a better world. The loss of God has meant the loss of what it means to be human. Moral issues are being decided with a relativistic mind-set. To add to our woes we are faced with the sexual abuse scandal within our own ranks. Victims of abuse have experienced a profound betrayal of trust. The pastors of the Church have lost credibility in the eyes of many. Besieged from within and from without by forces that threaten destruction, the Barque of Peter could appear to be sinking. But down through history, at times like this, when all seems so dismal, the Holy Spirit has been poured out afresh, generating a new springtime of renewal. These are undoubtedly troubled times but they are not times to despair. The good news is that we are living in an era of a new Pentecost within the Church, a new outpouring of the Holy Spirit for the sake of personal holiness and a new evangelization.

A Personal Pentecost

In this book I don't intend to address ecclesial issues. Rather I am going to focus on the activity of the Holy Spirit in the life of the individual believer. This will involve at times speaking about the

Church community of faith and love, since "no person is an island"; we all belong to one another in the Body of Christ. However, my focus is on the way the Holy Spirit anoints us as individuals, bringing personal conversion and transformation of life. Nevertheless a renewed Church will be built primarily from the changed hearts of those who have experienced a new outpouring of the Holy Spirit in their lives. It will be dependent on individual Catholics experiencing a new personal Pentecost. To the extent that individual conversions happen we will collectively create a new culture of Pentecost in the Church, which will bear fruits of holiness and evangelization.

I am writing this work from my own personal experience of the Holy Spirit's activity in my life and the lives of others in and through the Charismatic Renewal. I am thoroughly convinced that the gift of what is called in the Renewal "the baptism in the Holy Spirit" is a huge grace being given to the Church in these days. This grace in its broadest understanding is for all members of the Church, since it is fundamentally a renewal of one's sacramental Baptism and Confirmation. Being "baptized in the Spirit" is the core experience of the new Pentecost for the Church.[1] When we open ourselves to this grace we discover a new awareness of the Spirit's activity in our lives, and become more expectant of this activity. This is an experience which all Catholics, as a result of sacramental Baptism, inherently desire.

Through sacramental Baptism we receive the Holy Spirit to become sons and daughters of God, and in Confirmation we receive the Holy Spirit to become witnesses of Jesus to others. However, the graces of these sacraments can lie dormant within our lives. Some Catholics may go through their whole life journey without ever experiencing this renewal in the Spirit. That would be a great loss. The gift of the Spirit which we already received in the sacraments of initiation needs to be stirred up in a new way. St Paul says, "Fan into a flame the gift God gave you when hands were laid upon you ..."(2 Tim 1:6). The power inherent in our Baptism and Confirmation needs to be released so these sacraments can be more fruitful in our lives.

Seraphim of Sarov said that the whole Christian life is one invocation of the Holy Spirit. The whole goal of the life of a disciple is to be filled with the Spirit. We all need the graces of our Baptism and Confirmation to be awakened and released in us more powerfully. This doesn't have to manifest in us in a standardized way. Nor does it have to be at a single moment of time. However, a deliberate preparation over a period of time is the best way to make ourselves available for a new infilling of the Spirit. We first need to be evangelized; to hear the Good News of Jesus proclaimed, and to respond with repentance and faith. In my previous book, *Amazing Love*, I showed how the proclamation of the *kerygma* births faith. In response to this proclamation, if we commit our lives to Jesus, and surrender to him as Lord of our lives, we can then ask him to baptize us in his Holy Spirit. The grace of the baptism in the Spirit is given to us most richly when we truly surrender our lives to the Lord.

This gift is not exclusive to the Charismatic Renewal movement. It is for all Catholics. It is a big grace, available to all, and is not meant to be identified with any one group or movement. For this reason it is my hope that this book will not only be read by "card-carrying" members of the Charismatic Renewal, but also by all who are seeking to deepen in their experience of the Holy Spirit in their own personal lives. There is no group in the Church which can claim to have more of the Holy Spirit than others. In fact to make that claim would be prideful and elitist, and would surely grieve the Holy Spirit, whose genuine presence is always marked by humility and communion. The unique service that the Charismatic Renewal movement brings to the

Church is to create a greater awareness of the baptism in the Spirit, and humbly to help others discover this gift and prepare to receive it.

In the first two chapters I offer some background on the advent of the experience of the baptism in the Spirit within the Charismatic Renewal in the Catholic Church and discuss its importance for us today. I take this approach because from my personal experience I know no better way to demonstrate what is meant by a "new Pentecost". Then the rest of the work seeks to show what we can expect to happen in our lives if we yield to the Holy Spirit and are open to his action within us. Throughout the book I draw upon true testimonies of people whom I have known along the way. Only those names which include the surname are real. All other names of people, whose stories are included here, have been changed to protect their confidentiality. I am grateful to those who were willing to share their stories. I felt it was particularly important to include witnesses to the work of the Holy Spirit, since otherwise it all may sound too theoretical or even irrelevant.

I am grateful for the many people in various ecclesial movements and communities who witness to the grace of a "new Pentecost" in the Church today. I am particularly thankful for my long association within the Charismatic Renewal and worldwide fraternity of communities birthed in the Church out of the grace of the Renewal.[2] The new springtime in the Church which has come through the new outpouring of the Holy Spirit since the Second Vatican Council has given me hope in my journey of discipleship, and given new energy and vision for priestly life. With gratitude this book celebrates the lives of ordinary Catholics who are living in an extraordinary way a Spirit-filled life in imitation of Jesus for the sake of the gospel. Most of all it is a humble attempt to give glory to God for the action of the Holy Spirit in our lives, and to encourage all who read this book to open their lives to the Spirit, the Lord and Giver of life.

1
A NEW PENTECOST

I will pour out my Spirit upon all flesh, and your sons and your daughters shall prophesy, and your young men shall see visions, and your old men shall dream dreams (Joel 3:1).

Jesus Baptizes in the Spirit

The term "baptism in the Spirit" used in the Renewal today has been taken from the Scriptures, especially from John the Baptist, who identifies Jesus as "the one who baptizes in the Holy Spirit" (Jn 1:32-33). The biblical phrase is referring to the whole work of Jesus, as the Messiah. He is the one who "gives the Spirit without measure" (Jn 3:34), and has "poured out" his Spirit on all of redeemed humanity (Acts 2:33). Jesus promised this experience when he said to the apostles before ascending to the Father, "John baptized with water, but you will be baptized with the Holy Spirit not many days from now" (Acts 1:5). This promised outpouring of the Spirit would complete the work of the redemption. Jesus was referring to the gift of the Spirit at Pentecost.

It is important to understand that the verb "to baptize" in this context has a metaphoric sense: it means "to flood, to bathe completely and to submerge". It can be likened to plunging into a pool, because it involves a new immersion in the Holy Spirit. However, the term "baptism in the Spirit" is not referring directly to water Baptism, but refers more to the experience of the event of Pentecost. Yet it also suggests there is an intrinsic connection to the sacrament of Baptism, as I will explain more fully in the following chapter.³ We use the term in our times to speak of the grace of a *new* Pentecost, a new and sovereign outpouring of God's Spirit.

Witness of the Popes

In 1961 Pope John XXIII, when convoking the Second Vatican Council, prayed to the Lord to "renew your wonders in our time as by a new Pentecost".⁴ His successor Pope Paul VI referred to this prayer as "a prophetic intuition" which he experienced as already being fulfilled. The fruit of the Council, he claimed, was "a work of the Spirit, a gift of Pentecost". He continued,

> Not that Pentecost has ever ceased to be an actuality during the whole history of the Church, but so great are the needs and the perils of the present ... that there is no salvation for it except in a new outpouring of the gift of God.⁵

In post-conciliar times the Church has gone through what Pope John Paul II called "a renewed outpouring of the Spirit of Pentecost". Addressing half a million people in St Peter's Square, representing over fifty renewal movements, on the eve of Pentecost 1998, he proclaimed with great passion and enthusiasm:

> The institutional and charismatic aspects are co-essential as it were to the Church's constitution. They contribute, although differently, to the life, renewal and sanctification of God's People. It is from this providential rediscovery of the Church's charismatic dimension that before and after the Council, a remarkable pattern of growth has been established for ecclesial movements and new communities ... you present here are a tangible proof of this outpouring of the Spirit.⁶

John Paul II saw the rediscovery of the charismatic dimension of the Church as the providence of God at work in this time of crisis. The new ecclesial movements and communities are clear evidence of this new outpouring of the Spirit of God for the sake of his Church and its mission. He went on to make an extraordinary plea to all members of the Church to open themselves to this new Pentecost:

> Today I would like to cry out to you all gathered here in St Peters Square, and to all Christians: Open yourselves docilely to the gifts of the Spirit! Accept gratefully and obediently the charisms which the Spirit never ceases to bestow on us![7]

Pope Benedict XVI also called for a new Pentecost. He chose the theme of World Youth Day 2008, "You will receive power when the Holy Spirit comes upon you, and then you will be my witnesses ..." (Acts 1:8). When reflecting on the significance of this text he invited the whole Church to experience being immersed in the Spirit:

> Today I would like to extend this invitation to everyone: let us rediscover, dear brothers and sisters, the beauty of being baptized in the Holy Spirit; let us be aware again of our Baptism and of our Confirmation, sources of grace that are always present. Let us ask the Virgin Mary to obtain a renewed Pentecost for the Church again today, a Pentecost that will spread in everyone the joy of living and witnessing to the Gospel.[8]

The Popes encourage us to build a "culture of Pentecost", a whole way of life which is deeply aware of the activity of the Holy Spirit and joyfully expectant of the promises of the Holy Spirit to be fulfilled in our lives. Pope John Paul II urged:

> In our time that is so hungry for hope, make the Holy Spirit known and loved. Help bring to life that "culture of

Pentecost" that alone can make fruitful the civilization of love ... never tire of praying 'Come Holy Spirit! Come! Come!'[9]

A New Outpouring of the Spirit

A retreat of some students and staff from Dusquesne University in Pittsburgh, USA, in 1967 is usually identified as the beginning of the Catholic Charismatic Renewal. Patti Gallagher Mansfield, one of the participants, testified to the surprising action of the Spirit, arriving at a time when they did not expect, yet coming in response to a deep yearning they had for the renewal of their sacramental Baptism and Confirmation. They had been reading the Acts of the Apostles and other books on the Holy Spirit. An expectancy had arisen in their hearts. They sang the *Veni Creator Spiritus* often, praying for the Spirit to come. Patti says she was so enflamed with desire for the Spirit that in her youthful enthusiasm she had written on the notice board for all to see: "I want a miracle!" During a birthday party on the Saturday night they were independently drawn to the chapel, and there before the Blessed Sacrament they experienced an immense sovereign outpouring of the Holy Spirit that was to change their lives. Patti received her miracle. This is how she described what happened to her on that night:

> As I knelt before the Lord Jesus Christ in the Blessed Sacrament, for the first time in my life, I prayed what I would call 'a prayer of unconditional surrender'. I prayed in the quiet of my heart, "Father, I give my life to you, and whatever you want of me, that's what I choose. If it means suffering, then I accept that. Just teach me to follow your Son, Jesus, and to learn to love the way He loves."
>
> When I prayed that prayer, I was kneeling before the altar.

The next moment I found myself prostrate, flat on my face, stretched out before the tabernacle. No one had laid hands on me. I had never seen such a thing happen before. I don't know exactly how it took place, but in the process, my shoes came off my feet. Later I realized that, like Moses before the burning bush, I was indeed upon holy ground. As I lay there, I was flooded from my fingertips to my toes with a deep sense of God's personal love for me ... His merciful love. I was especially struck by the foolishness of God's love. It is so completely undeserved, so lavishly given. There is nothing that you and I can ever, ever do to earn or merit God's love. It is freely given, generously given, out of the abundance of his mercy. Our God is a God of love. He created us out of love and destined us for love. We are his people. We belong to him. His love is for us no matter what we've done, no matter who we are.

As I think back over my experience in the chapel that night, the words of St Augustine so beautifully capture what I felt in those moments: "You have made us for yourself, O Lord, and our hearts are restless until they rest in you." Within me echoed the fervent plea, "Stay! Stay! Stay!" I felt as if I wanted to die right then and go to be with God in Heaven. Yet I knew that if I, who was no one special, could experience the love and mercy, the tenderness and compassion of God in such a way, it was possible for anyone, yes anyone, to experience God as well. Although I just wanted to remain and bask in the presence of the Lord, I knew that I needed to share this experience with others. Like the apostles after Pentecost, I wanted to "proclaim his marvelous deeds", to give witness to the Living God.

That one brief encounter with the Lord taught me more than a lifetime of study could ever have done. I felt myself captivated by the beauty and goodness of the Living God. The mercy and love of Jesus had overwhelmed me.[10]

Not everyone who asks for the baptism in the Spirit will experience the overpowering presence of God in a palpable way. The actual experience at the moment of being prayed over for the Spirit is not so important. It will vary in intensity. For some it will be simply a quiet peace and sense of God's tender love. For others it may be more outwardly dramatic. But this is of little consequence. What really matters is the change that happens afterwards in our lives. When we experience the new fire of the Holy Spirit at work in our lives, all is made new. One of the participants on that Dusquene weekend wrote a letter to a friend a few days later. This is how he summed up what had happened:

> Our faith has come alive, our believing has become a kind of knowing. Suddenly, the world of the supernatural has become more real than the natural. In brief, Jesus Christ is a real person to us, a real person who is Our Lord and who is active in our lives. We read the New Testament as though it were literally true, now, every word, every line. Prayer and the sacraments have become truly our daily bread instead of practices which we recognize as 'good for us'. A love of Scripture, a love of the Church I never thought possible, a transformation of our relationships with others, a need and a power of witness beyond all expectation, have all become part of our lives. The initial experience of the baptism in the Spirit was not at all emotional, but life has become suffused with calm, confidence, joy and peace ...[11]

Since that weekend an estimated 120 million Catholics spread over 220 countries have experienced the baptism in the Spirit within the ministry of the Charismatic Renewal. Testimonies differ. However there are some characteristic features of this conversion which are commonly reported. People experience a new revelation of Jesus as their loving Saviour, and new depth of surrender to Christ as Lord, a deep infilling of the love of God, a new ability to call God, "Abba", a new love for Scripture, for the Sacraments, and for the Church, a new hunger to learn the teachings of the Church, a new inspiration to praise and worship God from the heart, a new desire for personal holiness, a new power to change sinful patterns and to develop in a life of virtue, a new capacity to love others and a desire to live the communal life of the Church, a blossoming of charismatic gifts, a new love for the poor, a deeper healing of the heart and deliverance from bondage to evil, a new fire and boldness in evangelization, and a new desire for unity in the Church. What faithful Catholic would not want these fruits in one's life?

A Personal Journey

My own experience of this "big grace" was decisive for my life, but not at all emotionally dramatic. My personal Pentecost took place when some young people convinced me to go on a priests' charismatic retreat which was preached by a Redemptorist, Fr Tom Forrest. At the time Fr Tom was heading up the International Charismatic Renewal Office in Rome. In a key talk in the retreat Fr Tom, in inimitable style, threw out a challenge: "You need to be able to say three words …" There was a dramatic pause, and I was wondering, what were these three words. Then he slowly and emphatically pronounced these words that were so important, "I CAN NOT!" As priests we can think we are in control of things, and that we just need better pastoral planning, better programs, better liturgical reforms, better teaching of catechism, better human development projects, etc., and then we will renew the Church. Fr Tom was saying that, as good as these efforts may be, we will never get anywhere unless we first admit our helplessness, our weakness, our incapacity, our nothingness without God. Providentially, I was at that moment in my life when I was vulnerable to this message. I knew that I had been self-sufficient in my ministry, and I had been a priest long enough to have experienced dismal failure in well-planned pastoral projects. I also was struggling to gain order in my own personal life. I didn't have a way of going forward in ministry, nor did I have a way of going forward in my own personal call to holiness.

Then the preacher went further, "you need to be able to say one more word: "YES!" That is, "Yes, Lord, you can!". He was inviting us to an attitude of surrender to the Lord; to adopt the response of Mary to the angel's message, when she was faced with the impossible, "Let it be done to me according to your will." We were invited to yield with Mary to the overshadowing of the Holy Spirit. We were encouraged to use the prayer of abandonment of Charles de Foucauld, and surrender our lives to the "big grace" of the baptism in the Spirit. When I was prayed over I experienced a quiet peace that descended upon me, and I knew that I was in the Lord's hands, and available for him to move me as he wished. The fruits of that surrender to the Spirit's power in my life became evident immediately in a new freedom for a life of virtue, and also in a whole new movement of the Spirit in ministry that gave new power in preaching and the manifestation of the gifts of the Spirit.

Moved by the Holy Spirit

Some years ago I was with leaders of charismatic communities from around the world visiting some of the dicasteries in the Roman curia. We had the opportunity of having time with Cardinal Ratzinger, who at that time was Prefect of the Congregation for the Doctrine of the

Faith. We were a little overawed being in the place where they used to condemn heretics to death. But our apprehensions disappeared when Cardinal Ratzinger appeared. He humbly listened to our reports of the Charismatic Renewal on every continent. Then he spoke to us in words similar to these. He said, "When I was a young priest I used to think that renewal in the Church would come about through better planning and programs." But he added, "Now I am older I know that it will happen through prayer and the Holy Spirit." He thanked us for sharing on the power of prayer and Holy Spirit, and begged us to continue. Not knowing that we were speaking with a future Pope, the leader of the group asked the Cardinal whether we could pray over him. To my astonishment he humbly agreed, and we extended our hands towards him and prayed. His silent witness spoke to me that the fundamental position of the Church and of all its leaders is to be in humble surrender to the Spirit of God.

This reminds me of a humorous story told of Pope John XXIII, who was renowned for his winning smile and jovial attitude to life. The Pope was visiting the Holy Spirit Hospital in Rome. The Mother Superior of the Sisters who ran the hospital was in quite a flap with the Pope arriving. She greeted the Pope and blurted out, "Welcome, Holy Father, I am the Superior of the Holy Spirit." Without missing a beat the Holy Father responded, "Well you have one up on me. I am only the Vicar of Christ!"

Whether the story is apocryphal or not, it may serve as a humorous reminder not to become the "superior of the Holy Spirit". The attitude we need to adopt is rather docility to the Spirit, surrendering to his work in our lives, yielding to his movement. In John's gospel we are told by Jesus, "The wind blows wherever it pleases. You hear its sound, but you cannot tell where it comes from or where it is going. That is how it is with all who are born of the Spirit" (Jn 3:8). We can detect the wind by its effects, by its sound or by its movement on the trees. But we do not see the wind itself. And just as we cannot control the wind, so we cannot control the Holy Spirit. Cardinal Suenens, who was a great friend of the Renewal, using a yachting image, used to say, "Put up your sail, and make sure you are downwind of the Holy Spirit." St Paul says, "Everyone moved by the Spirit is a child of God" (Rom 8:14). This is the distinguishing feature of genuine children of God. Rather than being moved solely by our own intelligence, ingenuity, will-power or natural desires, we are more true to our Baptismal identity when we are led by the Spirit, and motivated by his promptings.

Wind Surfing in the Spirit

Sr Bernadette had entered the convent when she was seventeen. She was a highly competent and dedicated religious. It so happened that after twenty years in ministry as a nun she had contact with a heroin addict who was facing trial for drug abuse. The chief of the police drug squad invited her to come to the court case to support the parents of the addict. During the trial the defendant sent her a message asking her to visit him in prison. She accepted the invitation and faithfully visited the young man for months, trying to influence him to change. But nothing was happening. All the prayers she made for him seemed to be ineffective, and all her talking seemed to meet deaf ears. One day he said to Sister, "If I could promise you that I could give up drugs I would, but I can't." She felt helpless and was beginning to despair. As much as she wanted to assist him, it seemed nothing was working.

Through a series of circumstances not initiated by Sr Bernadette, God began to work. The prisoner had been released on parole. A number of Spirit-filled people turned up, and began to take turns in praying over him in four hour shifts around the clock. He opened himself up and was filled with the power of the Spirit, and gave up drugs completely! This had a huge impact on Sr Bernadette's life. Prior to this she "had filed away anyone who was charismatic under 'C' for crackpot". The witness of this man's healing inspired her to attend a charismatic retreat. She was prayed over for the Holy Spirit and everything changed in her life. In her own words, "The only way I can describe the difference is that, for those who know about wind surfing, it was like for forty-three years of my life I had only been using the board to sit on. Suddenly I was now standing up, and the wind of the Holy Spirit had caught the sails of my life, and I took off with the Holy Spirit. Thus began the great adventure of my life."

In the following week Sister Bernadette was assigned the task of running a parish where there was no resident priest. The retiring priest, who knew Sister well, had warned the parishioners she would not be able to speak to them, as it would be beyond her to do so. She remembers that Ash Wednesday Communion service well. After reading the Gospel, she launched into a reflection. "My words surprised me. I can remember feeling as if the old me was standing over in the corner saying 'Wow'. I felt so strongly that the Holy Spirit was leading me to be bold, just like the first Apostles." And it would be true to say she hasn't stopped proclaiming the word since. She testifies that "the scales fell from my eyes" as she had new insight from the bible; a new fire of love drawing her more deeply into personal prayer; and new power of the Spirit giving her victory over previously sinful areas in her life.

Trusting in the Spirit

It is easy for good religious people to domesticate the work of the Holy Spirit. The new insights of psychology, sociology and other human sciences have been an enormous gift to the Church, both in the spiritual life and in ministry. However, being equipped with professional qualifications in these disciplines, can subtly lead us to think that we are self-sufficient in our own personal growth and in ministry. We lose an awareness of the supernatural action of God. We can grind on stoically in our daily slog, not really moving in the power of the Holy Spirit. We enter each day with the "business as usual" attitude, making our plans and strategies, coming up with ideas and visions, ploughing ahead industriously. But how much of all this output of energy is inspired by the Spirit? The phenomenon of "burn-out" is undoubtedly a complex reality, but, is it possible that sometimes a major contributing factor is that we are moving more in the flesh than in the Spirit, more by our own designs than by the purpose of God?

Fr Chris Ryan, who was responsible for the journey of the World Youth Day Cross and Icon throughout Australia in 2008, relates how often people of all ages and stages would be visibly moved by the Cross. At the moment of touching, kissing or embracing the Cross it was not unusual for people to weep, or in some way to be touched, maybe because in that moment they realized their need to go to Confession or maybe they were just grateful for the love of Christ who died for them, or maybe it was a moment of personal encounter with the Lord that came as a surprise. He noted that often the depth of people's responses seemed to be out of proportion to the simplicity of the gestures being made. He was aware that all sorts of psychological and sociological explanations may be given for this. But at the deepest level, he reflects, it was undoubtedly the action of the Holy Spirit:

> The memory serves now to remind me that the greatest need of the Church in Australia at this time is not a great

new program or strategic plan. There is an abundance of wonderful programs and plans. They are necessary and have their place. But too often we think that we have to make it happen; too often we act as if it all relied upon us. It doesn't all rely upon us: it all depends completely upon the Spirit. Nothing of consequence will be built and nothing of lasting good will be done unless it is done in cooperation with the Spirit of God. Programs are not, and can never be, a replacement for radical reliance upon the Spirit of God. It is really only the Holy Spirit who can touch hearts and transform lives. If the Church in Australia is to be renewed then it will be because we have allowed ourselves to be guided by the Spirit and trusted in his action in the world.[12]

2

RENEWAL OF BAPTISM

Rekindle the gift of God that is within you through the laying on of hands; for God did not give us a spirit of cowardice, but rather a spirit of power and of love and of self-discipline (2 Tim 1:6).

The Lord is moving in a sovereign way in today's Church to meet our current crisis. We used to be able to assume that cradle Catholics, even if they wandered from the faith during their teenage and young adult years, would make their way back after marriage and settle down. We presumed that the Catholic school was probably going to catch them when the kids arrived, and they would be set back on track. We can no longer presume that the Catholic identity is as resilient as it may have been in the time of "cultural Catholicism". Young Catholics are not going to Mass anyway, and many are choosing not to marry. Why would they bother to raise their children as Catholics? We can no longer depend on sacramental moments, or family pressure, or cultural expectations to keep people in the Church. We cannot presume that a Catholic identity nurtured during childhood is going to endure through the test of the current culture of widespread abandonment of Christianity. Add to this the attempt by many to sideline the Catholic Church to the fringes of society as a quaint museum piece, reminiscent of the grand cathedrals of Europe, that so often are bustling with gaping tourists, but left empty of worshippers.

What is God Doing?

The majority of people who migrate from the Catholic faith fall roughly into two main categories. They either join the growing statistical grouping of the "unaffiliated", or they become enthusiastic adherents of an evangelical brand of Christianity. What is the reason for this?[13]

Often Catholics may be practising their faith, and be quite active in parish organizations, but they do not enjoy a living personal relationship with Jesus. Many do not even seem to have a concept of a personal God, who is deeply concerned about them, and desires relationship with them. Those who drift away from the Catholic faith may easily be drawn into the secularized void, or even become proponents of an atheistic creed. However, many find their spiritual search leads them surprisingly to evangelical Protestants or Pentecostals. There they find what the heart was longing for – a personal relationship with Jesus. They realize what they had not been shown in the Catholic system – that we have a personal loving God, who sent his Son to die for our salvation, and that he calls us to open our hearts to him so he can draw us into union with him. They discover Jesus as their Saviour and Lord, and they discover what it means to be a disciple of Jesus. They are given the opportunity to be an intentional disciple, by developing a personal prayer life, a love for the Scriptures, a freedom of worship, a new hope for living, a sense of belonging within a warm fellowship of Christians, who support one another and encourage one another in the faith.

What then is God doing in the Renewal movements since Vatican II, and even before? What is he doing in the Charismatic Renewal through this "big grace" called the baptism in the Spirit? He is providing a way for genuine adult conversion to take place, a way for Catholics to be released in the power of their Baptism, for them to come to know Jesus personally, and to discover the inherent power of the basic gospel message. He is stirring Catholics to come alive in the Spirit, to fall in love with Jesus, and to bring joyfully the Good News of Jesus Christ to others.

The Sun had Risen in Me

Derek grew up in what he terms a "staunch Catholic family". He remembers nostalgically as a child praying the family Rosary, mandatory Sunday Mass, and the discipline of Catholic schooling. However, when he was in Years 11 and 12, and then later in college years, he drifted away from the practice of the faith. He was trialling for the St Kilda Under 19s and thoroughly immersed in Aussie Rules footy culture; drinking heavily, and indulging in disordered relationships with women. Being well built and large in stature, he was undefeated in pub fights. Yet at college he still managed to do well academically, and set out to build a career in business and finance. This took him to another city where he felt a terrible loneliness. To assuage the pain he married quickly at the age of 23. Three years later his wife ran off with another bloke, leaving him devastated. Moving back to Melbourne he was still plagued by loneliness, and tried desperately to find comfort in alcohol and women. He says it was like being caught in a whirlpool – you start off at the edges, and gradually you are helplessly sucked down and destroyed. He would look in the mirror and didn't know who he was anymore.

Meanwhile Derek's dear mother was praying for him, and urging him to go to Mass: "The nightclubs and pubs are not good for you. You will meet the right girl in the church." Derek had been granted an annulment from his first attempted marriage, and was desperate to find a woman to marry. But he did not heed his mother's advice. He was oppressed under the heavy weight of anxiety and a sense of abandonment. At the age of 33 years there seemed no way ahead for him. One night in his townhouse the depression was so severe that he physically collapsed to the floor. He thought he was going to die. In this lowest moment, close to despair, he cried out to God. He says he did not know where the words came from, but it was a prayer from the heart, "God, I can't do this anymore. You have to be first." His Mum, realizing this was a turning point, told him to see a priest. Derek made his confession for the first time in many years.

Then his Mum invited him to a Life in the Spirit Seminar. Derek recalls that when he was prayed over for the baptism in the Spirit, it was a peaceful experience. But later when he was at home playing his guitar, "singing of how Jesus came to set us free, and died on the Cross for me" he experienced the Lord's love flow through him. "I felt like the sun had risen in me. Like a light that was warm and intense. I knew the Lord was with me. He loved me." Now Derek was at Mass often, and the Scriptures opened up to him. He "began talking with Jesus as a friend". He says "even nature came alive; I saw everything now in full colour". The veil over his eyes had been removed. His parish priest noticed the change, and invited him to play the guitar at the Sunday night Mass. On the first night he was a little nervous, when a lady came over and introduced him to Melanie who would like to help with the singing. It was love at first sight, and they were married two years later. Mum was right after all; he would find the girl meant for him at Mass. They now have six children and Derek has left behind him the world of high finance for a more modest income and a family-centred life, while giving generously in serving the Lord within the Church. During a time of reflective prayer Derek received an image that graphically describes his journey from darkness to light: "I had a picture of myself in a hole with no bottom. I was hanging on to the edge with my finger tips. Grotesque creatures were trying to pull me down. But a hand reached down into the pit and pulled me out. The hole closed up behind me. I looked up. It was Jesus, who had lifted me up. He simply said, 'Come!'"

Releasing the Power of Baptism

The experience of being baptized in the Spirit makes real and reactivates our Baptism. That we need this experience is not saying there is anything defective about Baptism, as if the sacrament was deficient. Rather, it is highlighting the intrinsic power from God available to us through the sacrament of Baptism. The tragedy is that, for so many, the power of the sacrament has, as it were, been "tied", and consequently the sacrament cannot produce the power it is meant to have in our lives.[14] This can happen to any sacrament. If there are blocks within us, then a sacrament cannot bear the fruit it is meant to bear. So it can be with Baptism. While the sacrament has been celebrated validly, its power is still "unreleased".

Unfortunately, at least at the popular level, we have tended to think that the power of the sacrament of Baptism is guaranteed once we have made sure that the ritual has been performed validly. God will do the rest! But this is a defective way to view the effectiveness of a sacrament. Yes, the sacrament "works" if it is validly celebrated. But there is another side to sacramental experience which the Church teaches is also essential. This is the part the recipient of the sacrament plays.[15] If we are not aware, or just passive recipients, then the sacrament cannot bear fruit in our lives. For the sacrament to be powerful and fruitful in our lives we need to be disposed well beforehand, and also be consciously and actively drawing upon its power after its celebration.

Here is the rub! Most have received the sacrament of Baptism as children. Our parents and godparents stood for us and stated the faith for us. For the power of the sacrament to be released we need now as adults to do our part. And what is our part? It is personal faith in Jesus, preceded by repentance, in response to the gospel preached. "To all who received him he gave power to become children of God: to those who believe in his name" (Jn 1:13). Paul said to the Ephesians, who had received Baptism as adults, that Baptism was a seal upon their faith. First they had heard the word of the gospel, then they had responded by repentance and faith, and then they received the seal of the Spirit in their Baptism (Eph 1:13). Those who are preparing for adult Baptism have the amazing opportunity of standing under the word of God, consciously responding to this word in faith, and then being sealed in the Spirit through the waters of Baptism. If they are prepared well, and the sacrament is celebrated in a Spirit-filled way, their experience can be akin to that of the early Christians.

Need for Conversion

For the first six to eight years of the Church the experience of adult initiation was in itself a palpable infilling of the Spirit and a manifestation of charisms.[16] In adult Baptism the sacramental action and the personal surrender in faith of the person receiving the sacrament can be synchronized. The fullness of the sacrament of baptism is manifest. But for most of us who were "born Catholic" these two aspects of the sacrament, the ritual celebration and the personal "yes" in faith, have been separated by a long space of time. This is why the renewal movements in the Church today are all in some way seeking to renew our Baptism. And it is certainly why the Lord in his mercy has given the "big grace" of the baptism in the Spirit through the Charismatic Renewal to the Catholic Church at this time in history.

In earlier days when children were ensured a Christian environment with a closed social grid of Catholic culture, an environment which was fully supportive of faith, then the faith response that completes the experience of Baptism emerged gradually over time. Even today, when we are in a more hostile environment to Christian beliefs and values, families and communities manage to gradually elicit the faith response from their children. Yet given our new cultural situation the chances are much higher that there will be a rupture in this process of "cultural osmosis". In today's world it is rare for a baptized Christian to grow by nurture alone into a mature faith response to Jesus, and to be so moved by the Spirit to be able to freely declare "Jesus is Lord!" We need to do all we can to enhance the nurturing of faith through catechesis, sacramental programs, and especially through family influence. But the movement into adult years can be so tumultuous in today's cultural climate we need as well an intentional strategy of offering Catholics the opportunity of personal conversion involving a decision for Christ and a readiness to become his disciple.[17]

The baptism in the Spirit is God's response to the problem of Baptism losing its power and fruitfulness. When our Baptism is reactivated, its power is stirred up within us. We fan into a flame the gift that God has already given us (2 Tim:6-7). Until this moment the grace of the sacrament had been "tied". Now it is released in power.

Confirmation: Clothed in Power from on High

What about the sacrament of Confirmation? How does it fit into this schema? The sacrament of Confirmation can best be understood as intrinsically united with Baptism. Originally it was a post-baptismal anointing and laying on of hands by the bishop, which took place in the same integral ritual. By an accident of history, due to the lack of availability of the bishop, and the prevalence of infant baptism, Confirmation became separated from Baptism in the life of the individual.

The intrinsic theological unity between the two sacraments is based in the unity of the two mysteries of Easter and Pentecost. Baptism primarily initiates us into the Easter mystery, the death and resurrection of Jesus. Confirmation primarily initiates us into the mystery of Pentecost.[18] Just as Easter is geared towards Pentecost and would be incomplete without it, so Baptism is geared towards Confirmation and would be incomplete without it. Confirmation then confirms and opens up more fully the Pentecostal dimension of Baptism. This is why some groups have tried to prepare candidates for the sacrament of Confirmation so that it would be experienced as being baptized in the Holy Spirit. There is some merit in this pastoral approach, but it usually is not possible, since many Conferences of Bishops are not convinced that Confirmation should be delayed until adolescence or early adulthood, when the recipient could make an adult decision for the faith. They do not want Confirmation to be normatively an *adult* sacrament, when the Church remains committed to the importance of *infant* Baptism.

Whatever we might say about the on-going discussion around the appropriate age for Confirmation, for our purposes here it is sufficient to emphasize that everything which has been said about renewing the sacrament of Baptism can be said about the sacrament of Confirmation also. Usually for adults, who received both these sacraments as infants or children, the experience of being baptized in the Spirit is a releasing of the power of *both* sacraments. The graces of Baptism are remission of sin, becoming children of God, being regenerated in the Holy Spirit, being incorporated into the Body of Christ, and becoming part of the worshipping community. Confirmation confirms all of this, but emphasizes being "clothed with power from on high", filled with the Holy Spirit, for the purposes of being witnesses of the Good News of Jesus to the ends of the earth. The renewal of both these sacraments through the adult conversion experience of baptism in the Spirit opens up the intrinsic power in the Church for people to take on a genuine life of holiness and to receive the fire of the Spirit so they can share fully in the Church's fundamental mission of evangelization.

3
FIRE OF LOVE

Love is a flash of fire, a flame of the Lord himself. Love no floods can quench and not torrents drown (Song of Songs 8:6).

John the Baptist, speaking of Jesus, the Messiah, proclaimed, "I baptize you with water; but the one who is more powerful than me is coming ... He will baptize you with the Holy Spirit and fire" (Lk 3:16). This is the great promise which has now been fulfilled. Jesus *baptizes* us in the Holy Spirit. Being "baptized" means that we are filled to overflowing with the Spirit, immersed in the Spirit, saturated with the Spirit. And this experience fills us with the fire of God's love. The image of fire has many dimensions, but its strongest meaning in Luke's gospel is Love. Luke records Jesus exclaiming, "I have come to bring fire to the earth and I wish it were already blazing!" (Lk 12:49). This text gives insight into the heart of Christ; his desire for the fire of God's love to be experienced by all. The love he had burning in his heart, the love that was compelling him forward to the Cross, must through his suffering and death, make it possible for all hearts to be enflamed with this same self-sacrificing love. After hanging on the Cross with such amazing love, to win our hardened hearts to him, he has now returned to the Father. True to his promise, on the day of Pentecost, the Spirit was poured out upon the apostles and all those gathered in the upper room, with Mary, the Mother of Jesus, in their midst. Luke tells us that something appeared to them that appeared like tongues of fire, and rested on each of them. "All of them were filled with the Holy Spirit and began to speak in other languages, as the Spirit gave them the ability" (Lk 2:4). At Pentecost fire was cast to the earth. Since that time whenever the Spirit is poured out on human beings our hearts are enflamed with zeal for God, and love for others.

Transforming Fire

The Holy Spirit sets our hearts on fire with the gift of divine love. John proclaims, "God is love" (1 Jn 4:16). St Augustine comments, "Love presupposes one who loves, the one who is loved, and their love itself."[19] So, in the Triune God, the Father is the eternal lover, the Son is the one eternally loved, and reciprocates that love. The Holy Spirit is their love itself. So from all eternity the Father and Son have been loving one another, and the Holy Spirit proceeds as that Love. It is an only an analogy, but it helps us appreciate the gift of the Spirit. God's love could not be contained to himself, but by the very nature of love seeks union beyond itself. St Paul tells us, "God's love has been poured into our hearts through the Holy Spirit who has been given to us" (Rom 5:5). The Holy Spirit is Love itself. When he comes to us he sets us on fire with love for God and for our neighbour. We love God only because we have first received love *from* God. That is why John insists, "In this is love, not that we loved God but that he loved us, and sent his Son to be the atoning sacrifice for our sins" (1Jn 4:10). We love God because he has loved us first.

The Holy Spirit is the love of God, love in Person. When we read in the Pentecost account that "they were all filled with the Holy Spirit" this means that "they were all filled with the love of God!" Pentecost was not only a manifestation of the exterior power of God through a mighty wind and the room shaking. It was also a subjective event. They were inundated by love, "baptized" in love. Beforehand they had been cowering in fear behind closed doors, not sure of their future, and without courage to proclaim that Jesus of Nazareth is risen. But the experience of the overwhelming love of God changed that. "There is no fear in love; perfect love casts out all fear" (1 Jn 4:18). Now the great love story of the Church begins. The Church begins to carry in its heart the love story of Jesus, and cannot help but proclaim it. The fire of love that was in the heart of Christ, which took him to the Cross for our sake, is now poured out into the nascent Church. Love brings unstoppable power. Personally fired by the zeal of the Spirit, and no longer fearful of the consequences, they joined together in the joyful proclamation of the love of God made visible in Jesus Christ. They knew that nothing could come between them and this love. Later Paul, who had the same experience, expressed it well:

> Who will separate us from the love of Christ? Will hardship, or distress, or persecution, or famine, or nakedness or peril or sword? ... No, in all these things we are more than conquerors through him who loved us. For I am convinced that neither death, nor life, nor angels, nor rulers, nor things present, nor things to come, nor powers, nor height, nor depth, nor anything else in all creation, will be able to separate us from the love of God in Christ Jesus our Lord (Rom 8:35-39).

The Sign of the Spirit

The conclusive sign that we have received the Holy Spirit is not that one speaks in tongues, or prophesies or casts out demons or works miracles. Rather it is love of God and love of neighbour. We notice that St Paul, who highly favoured the charismatic gifts, says there is a way that is better than all of them (1 Cor 12:31). This is the way of love. The Church could easily be torn apart through gifted people being arrogant and competitive, in a way similar to the early Corinthian community. When the fire of God's love is genuinely poured out, and when this fire is burning in our hearts, granting us a passionate desire for union with God, we will also experience a new love for our neighbour, a new capacity to withdraw judgments, bestow forgiveness, seek reconciliation, and humbly serve the needs of others. The love of God and love of neighbor are two facets of the one gift of charity which comes from the heart of God.

Love seeks union. When God pours his Spirit into our hearts he is drawing us by his love into union with himself. He longs for us to be awakened in love for him. We may resist, but when we encounter Spirit-filled preaching of the *kerygma*, the proclamation of the truth of the death and resurrection of Jesus, the Spirit will open up our hardened hearts.[20] In response to the love of God manifest in the Cross of Christ, the Spirit calls us always to a deeper level of repentance and faith. We undergo a more profound conversion of heart, so we can respond with all our being in love for God. It is all the work of the Holy Spirit of fire, who enflames us with love.

Pope Paul VI declared that he was often asked about the greatest needs of the Church. What did he feel was the first and last need of the Church which he loved so much? His answer was this:

> We must say it, almost trembling and praying, because as you know well, this is the Church's mystery and life; the Spirit, the Holy Spirit. He it is who animates and sanctifies the Church. He is her divine breath, the wind in her sails, the principle of her unity, the inner source of her light and strength. He is her support and consoler, her source of charisms and songs, her peace and her joy, her pledge and prelude to blessed and eternal life. The Church needs her perennial Pentecost; she needs fire in her heart, words on her lips, prophecy in her

outlook ... the Church needs to rediscover the eagerness, the taste and the certainty of the truth that is hers ... And then the Church needs to feel flowing through all her human faculties a wave of love, of that love which is called forth and poured into our hearts 'by the Holy Spirit who has been given to us' (Rom 5:5).[21]

A Felt Experience

The most wonderful gift any human being can receive is to know that we are loved personally by God, who is Love. When we feel ourselves being drawn into the inner life of the Trinity, flooded with love, enfolded by love, overwhelmed by love, that is when we know fullness of life. We are most truly alive as human beings when we know we are embraced by God's love, when we feel his total acceptance of us as persons, whom he loves and has created for our own sake. Pentecost consists of this – a profound experience of the transforming love of God. Is it important that we *experience* it? And if we do can we trust these experiences? Some would say just receive it in the darkness of faith. Don't expect any experience! Undoubtedly the spiritual journey takes us eventually towards letting go of all sensory experiences, and standing in the darkness of deep contemplative prayer. However this should not dissuade us from opening up our lives to God, and letting him bring this Pentecost experience to us. If it was good enough for the apostles and the Blessed Virgin Mary it is good enough for us also.

The account of Pentecost in the Acts of the Apostles leaves us in no doubt that the initial infilling with the Spirit was a *felt experience* of significant proportions. After all people thought the apostles were drunk, even though it was only nine o'clock in the morning. This was a "sober intoxication in the Spirit",[22] but was not something hidden from others and not something without profound subjective experience.

As was said earlier, the baptism in the Spirit can be understood as providing the experiential dimension of our sacramental Baptism and Confirmation. It is often experienced as an adult conversion, when an individual provides living faith and a "yes" in surrender to the power of their sacramental Baptism and Confirmation. While the emotional content of the experience is not all that important, there is usually a level of tangible religious experience which accompanies this release of the Spirit. Our own personal Pentecost may not necessarily be an experience akin to drunkenness, but it will surely be *a touch of love*, a new fire within our soul which burns deeply for our personal transformation.

John says, "We have known and we believe the love that God has for us" (1 Jn 4:16). We don't only believe in God's love because we hold an intellectual conviction that God loves us. We believe by putting our *trust* in God's love. We come to *know* God's love. In the Scriptures to "know" is to experience in a personal way. The Scriptural evidence is that we ought to expect an experience of God's love, and it is not wrong to desire this experience. Although I hasten to add that if this baptism in the Spirit is to bear its full fruit it will take us on the contemplative journey. This will mean learning to live by faith and not by feelings, learning to fall in love with the Giver and not the gifts, learning to seek the God of all consolation rather than the consolations of God. Any journey of genuine discipleship will take us to the Cross, not only during our arid prayer times, but also in our life in the world.

I would also strike a note of caution that to expect a touch of God's love at the time of baptism in the Spirit is not to say that the indwelling of the Holy Spirit is always accompanied by tangible experience. In fact the usual manner of the Holy Spirit's mysterious activity in the soul is in a hidden, invisible manner involving no sensible experience at all. The Spirit's presence is known more by the fruits that are generated – love, joy, peace, patience, kindness, goodness, faithfulness, gentleness and self-control (Gal 5:22).

Becoming Fire

When John of the Cross spoke about immersion in the Holy Spirit he used the image of a log being penetrated by fire.[23] If the log has been damp, when the fire first touches it, some spiders and beetles may come rushing out. This could represent the deliverance from evil influences that may have to take place. Then we notice that the log oozes out some black fluid as it is dried by the fire and readied for burning. This could represent the need for repentance of sinful patterns and the dismissing of them from our lives. Then at a certain point we notice that the log ignites! It is on fire! This is the time of deeper purification and growth in virtue. It takes a long time for the fire to penetrate the log. However, if we wait long enough we finally notice that the log has been so filled with the fire that it is hard to tell the difference between the fire and the log. The log has *become* fire! The living flame of love is burning in our being, and in a sense our whole being is now suffused with the fire of God's love.

Whatever image we use to describe the process of being loved by God, and its impact on our lives, this is undoubtedly the most important dynamic for real human living. We are made for union with God, and his love at work within us by the fire of the Holy Spirit is meant to transform us into his likeness. This will mean that God becomes the passion of my life, and his love will flow freely through me for the sake of others. Just as in the Trinity the love between the Father and the Son does not end there, but continues in the Spirit, so also outside of the Trinity. The love of God is poured into us by the Holy Spirit, but it does not end in us. It fills us, and enflames us in such a way that we have the passionate love of God for others. We have a new fire which urges us to love in our turn. As John says, "Since God has loved us so much, we also ought to love one another" (1 Jn 4:11). With the experience of God's love we are lifted out of ourselves and empowered to transcend our selfish desires. We freely allow his love to flow through us.

Love Took Over My Life

Julia had been on a search for meaning in life. Although she had been brought up as a Catholic she no longer attended Mass, and was experimenting with other spiritual options. She tried Hinduism, Tibetan Buddhism, "New Age" healing rituals, crystals, and foot massaging, as well as dabbling in the occult out of curiosity. Every spiritual direction she turned left her feeling empty and worse than before she began. She started searching for God. Looking back she realizes now that she was burdened by low self-esteem, and had never felt good enough before others, not even her husband. She was jealous of gifts and possessions of others, who seemed to be more clever, more talented and more beautiful than her. Then in her early fifties she heard about a conference being conducted by Charismatic Renewal. She was highly sceptical, but she had read a book on healing by Fr Emiliano Tardif, who was to be one of the speakers at the conference. Encouraged by a friend she signed up to go. She was swept away by the loving Spirit-filled atmosphere of the conference, and on a given night was prayed over for the baptism in the Spirit.

After being prayed over she had a peace in her heart, yet she thought maybe she had been overlooked by God. But later that night, while lying in bed, she felt led to pick up her Bible. She opened it randomly to the account of Judas' betrayal of Jesus. It was as if she had been hit by a lightning bolt. She thought, "I am Judas! I had known Christ earlier in my life, and I betrayed him". She felt overwhelmed by fear as she realized who it was she had betrayed, and that he has the power to cast into hell. She wept and wept and wept. Then she remembered hearing about Peter who had betrayed Christ three times, and Jesus had forgiven Peter, who had discovered the mercy of God. Now she was on her knees pleading with the Lord to forgive her. As she prayed for mercy she was filled with a wonderful sense of God's total and unconditional love for her. She felt the Holy Spirit filling her to overflowing with his love. "This experience changed my life totally; love took over my life."

Back home after the conference she made a bonfire of all her books on numerology and other occult practices. She now experienced a deep joy in the Lord, and an ongoing sense of the love of God, which has never left her. In the light of his love she was free to be herself, and not to worry about what others may think of her or that she might be overshadowed by their gifts and talents. Now she felt lovable, and had power to love others. Not long after this her husband also was converted, and the Lord brought significant healing to their marriage. Julia found that the Lord had graced her with the charism of hospitality. For a number of years she and her husband opened their home to others who were seeking to find God in their life. Julia says, "After I had made all the preparations to receive people warmly, and was waiting for them to arrive, I just felt I was in the right place, at the right time, doing the thing I love doing most – welcoming people and letting them come to know God's love."

A River flowing

To change the analogy we could think of the inflowing of God's love as a river of life flowing from the side of Christ opened on the Cross for our sake. It is not meant to stop with our own experience of being loved. Rather, it is meant to be a river flowing through us to bring life to many others. A popular image to explain this is taken from the flow of the Jordan river. This famous river in the Holy Land forms two "seas", the Sea of Galilee and the Dead Sea. The Sea of Galilee receives the Jordan's water but then lets it flow out again. That sea is teeming with life. The Dead Sea, on the other hand, receives the Jordan's water but has no outlet. It keeps the water to itself; no streams flow out of it. It is truly "dead". There is no life in it; no fish in the sea and no vegetation on its shores. It is a salty wasteland. If we allow the experience of God's love in the Spirit, given us in Baptism, to be dammed up in ourselves, holding it all for ourselves, then we will be one of the many "walking dead". But if we allow the love poured into our hearts by the Holy Spirit to flow through us in favour of serving the good of others, we will be fully alive as God has intended.

A rather dramatic story from India can help to illustrate how God's love flows through us for others.[24] A husband and wife came to a charismatic retreat centre. The man was partially paralyzed and bound to a wheelchair. He had suffered a stroke a few years before and had become an invalid. He had to leave his job. She had to work to meet the expenses. The children were young and going to school. So she had to take care of her husband by herself. There was no government help available. Every evening she would return home from work tired, and do her many household chores and look after her husband's needs. Life was an endless cycle of exhausting work in her employment and in the family. She was depressed. Her husband had become a burden. The children were becoming too much. Life seemed impossible.

When they came for the five day retreat, this suffering couple finally had time to pray together. On the Wednesday evening during a Mass celebrated especially for couples she felt a great surge of love for her husband. She testified later that she had not felt so much love for her husband before, even when they were newly married and both healthy and everything was going well in their lives. As she felt this great current of love flowing through her, she felt prompted to lift her husband's hand which for years could not be moved. She felt this could be the time for healing. At that moment he was completely healed! The Holy Spirit has been described as the finger of God. And the finger of God moves in our lives by stirring us to love and to heal those around us. It may not always be as miraculous as that incident. But if we remain open to the infilling of God's love we can become beautiful instruments of bearing the power of his transforming love to others.

Love in Action

The primary fruit of the renewal in the Spirit should be practical love. The amazing story of Kkottongnae in Korea illustrates this beautifully. The name means "village of flowers", a small town built to care for psychiatric patients, people with physical and mental disabilities, the homeless and most abandoned people, and the dying. The founder of the whole complex, Fr (John) Woong-Jin Oh had already been baptized in the Spirit when he was a seminarian. He had started a prayer meeting in the basement of a hospital soon after the introduction of the Renewal movement to Korea, and as a deacon had experienced a Life in the Spirit seminar. The defining moment for Fr John's life came when just after his ordination as a priest in 1976 he saw a beggar passing by the church. He became curious and followed him. Reaching a cave in the mountainside Fr John discovered that the old man had been begging so he could carry food to a group of 18 people who lived in the cave, and were too weak to beg. That night in prayer, Fr John was inspired, "It is a grace of God even if you have strength to beg for food." He knew it was his vocation to reach out to the poor and abandoned who do not have the strength even to beg. The next morning he used the money he had, the equivalent of two dollars, and began to make bricks to build a house for the poor and abandoned. Others came to help, and soon he was able to bring all the abandoned people from the cave to live in what he appropriately named the *House of Love*.

In 1977 Fr John attended an overnight prayer meeting for priests and religious, fasting and praying all night for the outpouring of the Holy Spirit and spiritual gifts. Those who prayed over Fr John urged him to ask for the gift which he would need to live for the poor, and to help him live *with* the poor. Instead he says, "After hearing this I prayed just for the Holy Spirit, thinking that while there were many kinds of gifts, there is only one Holy Spirit who gives them to us." The next day while celebrating Mass he burst into tongues. On the Feast of the Assumption 1978 Fr John was driving across a bridge when he saw an old beggar in tattered clothes obviously dying. He stopped and took the man to the hospital. As he was doing so he heard the words from heaven, "I am glad and delighted you have saved my beloved son's life. I hereby propose a covenant. If you continue to accept such poor people in my name I will take care of everything else."

The Lord has been true to the covenant he made with Fr John. Now Kkottongnae has comprehensive welfare facilities. The community of love for the poor, made up of priests, religious, and lay people, has a vision for a world where no one feels abandoned, where all people are respected as created in the image of God, where we love one another as we love ourselves, and where people are prepared to sacrifice themselves for building a civilization of love. Kkttongnae also has a large centre for training people in the ministry of love, helping people to understand the results of love deficiency and how to meet that need. It also has a University of Social Welfare, training professionals from all over the world. In addition the original overnight prayer meeting which had sixteen people has morphed into a large centre for love and spirituality, where people are introduced through prayer to the Holy Spirit of love, drawing them into the heart of Jesus, broken open in love for the world.

4
LIGHT OF TRUTH

If you continue in my word, you are truly my disciples; and you will know the truth, and the truth will make you free (Jn 8:31-32).

Light to the Mind

The Holy Spirit's action within us illuminates the soul and opens the mind to the mysteries of God. St Paul says we teach "what no eye has seen, nor ear heard, nor human heart conceived, what God has prepared for those who love him". He then speaks about how we come to know these things:

> These things God has revealed to us through the Spirit; for the Spirit searches everything, even the depths of God. For what human being knows what is truly human except the human spirit that is within? So also no one comprehends what is truly God's except the Spirit of God. Now we have received not the spirit of the world, but the Spirit that is from God, so that we may understand the gifts bestowed on us by God ... interpreting spiritual things spiritually (1 Cor 2:9-13).

The Holy Spirit, who knows the inmost heart of God, gives us a wisdom from on high, which cannot be attained by human philosophy or ingenuity. The Spirit enlightens us about the truths of the faith, convinces us of the truth of who Jesus is, and brings the Scriptural word alive in a whole new way. A light is switched on within our minds and there is a new clarity and conviction of what has been revealed to us. Doctrine and dogmas are no longer dry, abstract, alien formulas but become immensely relevant and significant for our lives. The words of the Bible seem to lift off the page to speak personally to our situation. Jesus Christ is no longer a distant, historical figure of the past, who we may have learnt about in catechism classes. Now he is a real, alive person, the Son of God, who died for me and is risen, and is personally present to me. I no longer just know *about* him; I can truly say I *know* him. St Basil the Great put it this way:

> The Holy Spirit, power that sanctifies and light that gives understanding, himself grants to every rational creature the kind of clarity needed to discover the truth ... Just as one on whom the sunlight shines rejoices in it as if he (she) alone were touched by it ... so too is the Spirit present to each one able to receive him as though he (she) were the only one ... And just as something that is clear and transparent shines when a ray of light strikes it, and begins itself to give off light, so too the souls indwelt by the Spirit shine because of him, and made spiritual, begin to pour out grace upon others.[25]

The Holy Spirit brings new light to the mind which enables us to see in a new way. St Cyril of Jerusalem says:

> If someone has been in the dark and suddenly comes into the light of the sun, his bodily eye will keep the light and he will see clearly what he could not see before. In a similar way, someone who has been made worthy to receive the Holy Spirit will retain that enlightenment in his soul and in a way that transcends human nature will see things that could not be seen before.[26]

When we experience the Holy Spirit's activity we come to understand Divine Revelation more clearly and gain the wisdom of God. This is not only an intellectual grasp of the mysteries, but also a "taste" of what is revealed, an admiration and wonder at the beauty of God, a joyful grasp of the reality of who he is, and what he has done for us. It brings certitude of faith which is not arrogant or presumptuous, but humbly in awe of the mystery revealed.

A Quest for Truth

Mary Jo's Mum was a nominal Catholic and her father a nominal Anglican, but neither practised their faith. As she was growing up she remembers her parents being "hippies", searching for fulfillment in yoga, New Age healing weekends, having holidays in an Ashram, seeking guidance from astrology and crystal balls, and many other trendy spiritual pursuits. Oddly enough her parents sent her to a Catholic school. She was introduced to the sacraments, but they had no real attraction. By her teenage years she rebelled. She began to "hate" the Church, deploring what she perceived as hypocrisy, and was convinced the Church was against her. She even made a point of arguing publicly with Christian street preachers. She soon became fascinated with the occult, feeding on heavy metal, satanic music, and dressing in all black Gothic attire.

When she was fifteen her mother had a sudden conversion, and began to participate in charismatic prayer meetings. Mary Jo and her father poked fun at Mum ridiculing her for her new found faith in Jesus. But something began to happen in Mary Jo also, no doubt due to her mother's prayers. She discovered the *Lord of the Rings*, and loved it so much she read all of Tolkien's works. When she exhausted that, she started on C.S. Lewis' *Tales of Narnia*. After finishing school she travelled around the world for nine months, the last place she visited being India. This experience of Third World poverty shocked her to the core; she was confronted by her selfishness, realizing her hardness of heart, and her deep intellectual pride. Arriving back in Australia she read C.S. Lewis' *Mere Christianity*. A couple of sentences in the book hit home powerfully, "If Christianity is not true it is of no importance. If it is true than it is the most important thing you could ever know." She was convicted that she had dismissed Christianity out of prejudice. She needed to seek out whether it was real. She prayed to God, "If you exist, if you are real, I want to know you. I am confused about what is true. If Jesus is your Son, I want to know this." She had given God the opening.

She was still living the hedonistic life-style together with friends in an old warehouse, which doubled as a place to study and a music recording studio. But after her 21st birthday Mary Jo fell into deep depression. One night while in bed, feeling completely abandoned and alone, as if the world was in total darkness, and no else existed in the entire universe, she felt the presence of personified Evil taunting her, "There is nothing else! Just come to me!" Terrified she cried out to God, "How can you bear to see me like this. Help me!" Then the phone rang. It was her Mother, who was downtown at a prayer meeting, ringing to persuade Mary Jo to come join her. "There is an exciting visiting speaker about to preach." Mary Jo slammed the phone down. Then it rang again. She ignored it. But then with the phone ringing for the third time, she realized that maybe this was God's answer to her prayer. She drove to the prayer meeting in a daze. Arriving she found herself welcomed so warmly and lovingly that she wanted to cry, but resisted defiantly. She felt so conspicuous in her army boots, tights with holes, petticoat on the outside, black finger nails, and black lips. But during the preaching she just felt the presence of Jesus asking gently, why are you resisting? She let it all go, surrendered to the tears, finding the courage for a moment to be her broken self. She sobbed and sobbed and sobbed. But still this was but a moment of openness. She was not yet surrendered to the Lord. But since an opening had been made, the Spirit began to move in new ways.

Living in the country Mary Jo found the Lord speaking to her through creation. After dreaming of a freak storm affecting the family home, she was taken aback when the storm actually happened as she had dreamt it. She was drawn to the passage in the Psalms, "God speaks through the storm." She began to sense that God was speaking to her. She responded, "OK, God, I am listening." Seeing how God was showing his power and glory through the storm, she became aware of her arrogance, "How dare I address the God of the storm." But then she realized his love and his gentleness. While he has power to destroy, he chooses not to do so. She decided to believe. She was following the text, "Blessed are those who have not seen, yet believe" (Jn 20:29). But her heart was not yet touched. She knew there must be more. She started praying for faith from the heart.

One day while vacuuming the carpet in her parents' home, she was weeping in frustration and sorrow over her incapacity to have faith. At that moment she experienced an infilling of the Holy Spirit. She began to shout, "It's true! It's true!" She immediately began praying in tongues. Overnight she threw off the Gothic black clothes, and began to wear white, symbolizing her new awareness of being a daughter of God. "I now *knew* Jesus is the truth. I *knew* that Jesus died for me, and that he had risen from the dead. Now this was the most important reality in the whole world! Jesus was everything! From that moment everything centred on him, on being in relationship with him. I *knew* him. He began transforming my life. That moment I met Jesus who is the truth. The joy flooded my heart. I was now weeping for joy."

Promise of the Spirit of Truth

In the Last Supper discourse in John's Gospel Jesus four times promises the Holy Spirit, who will come to bring assurance to the apostles after he has returned to the Father. All four references are to the Spirit of truth. He says, "I shall ask the Father, and he will give you another Advocate to be with you forever, that Spirit of truth whom the world can never receive" (Jn 14:16). The term "Advocate" has a number of meanings, but in this context it speaks most of the interior witness of the Spirit, who teaches us the truth of who Jesus is. Next Jesus says to his apostles, "I have said these things to you while still with you; but the Advocate, the Holy Spirit, whom the Father will send in my name, will teach you everything" (Jn 14:26). The light of the Holy Spirit instructs us at a level beyond the ordinary grasp of reflective reasoning. The Spirit speaks to us at the intuitive level of knowing. Without this illumination we would be bereft of a true understanding and appreciation of what Jesus intends us to know. Jesus also said, "When the Advocate comes whom I shall send to you from the Father, the Spirit of truth who issues from the Father, he will be my witness" (Jn 15:26). When we hear the word of God in preaching, or read the word of God in the Scriptures, the Holy Spirit witnesses in the mind and the heart to the truth of what is heard or read, and pierces the mind, opens the heart, and brings conviction.

The final reference in the discourse seems to sum up all that has already been said, and assures us that his return to the Father does not leave us orphans without a teacher any more. Much to the contrary, his return to the Father means we will receive the Holy Spirit as our teacher, who will give us the way to interpret all that Jesus has said and done.

> I still have many things to say to you but they would be too much for you now. But when the Spirit of truth comes he will

lead you to the complete truth, since he will not be speaking as from himself but will say only what he has learnt; and he will tell of the things to come. He will glorify me, since all he tells you will be taken from what is mine (Jn 16:12-14).

The Spirit reveals Jesus

We need to note that the purpose of the Spirit is to glorify Jesus. The Spirit convinces us of what Jesus has done for us in his death and resurrection. The Spirit pierces the mind with the truth of the saving death of Jesus, and shows us the full extent of his amazing love for us. Often when people experience the baptism in the Spirit they gaze upon the crucifix with new eyes of faith. Beforehand they may have been afraid of the sufferings of Jesus, or maybe felt somehow alienated from the Cross. While feeling a desire to understand the meaning of the Cross, they may have found it difficult to penetrate the mystery of why this man would die for us. But now through the revealing action of the Spirit they are overwhelmed by the love manifest by Jesus through his passion and death, and will spend hours gazing upon the crucified Christ with tears of sorrow for their sins, with deep gratitude for the gift of his sacrifice for us, and with heartfelt love for Jesus, our Saviour.

While the Holy Spirit awakens the heart to the meaning of the death of Jesus, he also awakens the heart to the significance of the resurrection. When people experience the Spirit in a new way they invariably have a new exhilaration as they discover that "Jesus is Lord!" Previously they may have spoken about him as "Our Lord", referring affectionately to the historical Jesus in the gospels. But it is a whole new revelation to be able to say with deep conviction, "Jesus Christ is Lord!" When we proclaim that Jesus Christ is Lord we are deeply aware, due to the penetration of the Holy Spirit, that Christ is risen. He is alive! He is no longer just the object of devotion that we remember from the gospel stories, but now due to the enlightenment of the Holy Spirit, he is a living personal reality, the Risen Christ whom we encounter with living faith. This is why St Paul says, "No one can say, 'Jesus is Lord' except by the Holy Spirit" (1 Cor 12:3).

St Paul exclaims, "I believe nothing can happen that will outweigh the supreme advantage of knowing Christ Jesus, my Lord" (Phil 3:8). This is a marvellous proclamation. He later cries out with full conviction, "All I want is to know Jesus Christ and the power of his resurrection ..." So all that matters in life, regardless of our circumstances, is that we know Jesus Christ, and that we acknowledge him to be the Lord. This is what brings salvation. He says elsewhere, "If you confess with your lips that Jesus is Lord, and believe in your heart God raised him from the dead you will be saved" (Rom 10:9). All of this is the work of the Holy Spirit. No amount of study can produce this revelation. Fr Raniero Cantalamessa, preacher to the Papal household under both John Paul II and Benedict XVI, gives his testimony to this:

> I used to teach the history of Christian origins at the Catholic University of Milan. My doctoral thesis in theology was on the Christology of Tertullian, and the study of Christological doctrines of antiquity continued to be the main focus of my research and my teaching. Yet I became aware of something that made me uneasy. When I was speaking of Jesus in the lecture halls, he became a subject of research. As in all historical research, the researcher needs to master his subject and remain neutral in regard to it. But how could it be possible to "master" this subject and how would it ever be possible to remain neutral toward it? How could one reconcile that with the Jesus one called on in prayer and received each morning in the Eucharist?

The discovery of Jesus as "Lord" that came to me along with the baptism in the Spirit wrought a great change that I would never have been able to achieve by myself alone. It seemed to me that I became able to see what lay behind Saint Paul's experience, when all at once he began to consider as 'disadvantage' all the things that before he had looked upon as 'advantages' he had enjoyed in life, and as 'so much rubbish' everything other than "the supreme advantage of knowing Christ Jesus my Lord". I saw all at once what boundless gratitude, what pride and joy were hidden in that phrase of his, in that pronoun in the singular, "Christ Jesus *my* Lord".

I knew so many things about Jesus: doctrines and heresies and explanations ancient and new. But when I read Paul's exclamation in this context, "I want to know him" (Phil 3:10), that simple little "him" seemed to me to contain infinitely more than all the books I had ever read or written. For Christ is in fact the living Jesus, the risen one who is alive in the Spirit: not theories and doctrines about Jesus, but Jesus himself ... There is a difference between the real, living Jesus and the Jesus you find in books and learned discussions about him; it is the same as the difference between the real sky and a penciled sketch of the sky on a piece of paper.[27]

Scripture Comes Alive

The Holy Spirit brings the Scriptures alive. Reading the Bible without the Holy Spirit is like trying to read a book in a dark room. We need the light of the Holy Spirit. The Constitution on Divine Revelation of Vatican II (*Dei Verbum*) said the Bible "must be read and interpreted with the help of the same Spirit through whom it was written".[28] It is not like any other book, which may be read and understood simply by the light of natural reasoning. Because it was written under the inspiration of the Spirit, and conveys the word of God intended for our salvation, it must be read prayerfully and its meaning revealed by the light of the Holy Spirit. Over the years I have been amazed at the way people who are imbued with the Spirit of God, but have no formal learning, can understand the meaning of a text and teach upon it with "authority". The Holy Spirit reveals the secrets of God to "little ones". Of course, the apostolic authority of the Church's Magisterium is the ultimate guide for true interpretation of Scripture. But here we are talking about the meaning *for us*, the more existential experience of the Biblical word, which has power to change our lives by its impact upon us. Here we are not so much seeking to grasp the literal meaning of the text; rather we are submitting with humble and docile hearts to the word, asking the Holy Spirit to yield its present meaning *for us*. Rather than use some form of analysis to attempt to interpret the word, we prayerfully allow the word to interpret us.

At this more informal level of individual prayer and sharing groups the Spirit moves to open up the Scriptural word to speak into our lives personally. The Holy Spirit makes the word given in Scripture a personal communication of God to us. We are encouraged by *Dei Verbum* that in the Scriptures "the Father who is in heaven comes lovingly to meet his children and talks with them".[29] God the Father does not communicate to us as if the Bible was like a mimeographed letter written to everyone, or an email sent out to the masses. Even though everyone who picks up the Bible will read the same words on the page, when we read it in the light of the Spirit, the message conveyed is extraordinarily personal. It is very much like receiving a love letter just written for you. The word speaks into your own individual situation bringing comfort and challenge, direction and guidance.

Listening with Hearts Burning

The Holy Spirit continues today what the Risen Christ did with the disciples on the road to Emmaus. The two disciples were walking away from Jerusalem, bitterly disappointed, defeated and disillusioned. Their hopes were dashed. When Jesus came to walk alongside them they did not recognize him. At his questioning they recounted the sad turn of events in Jerusalem about the death of Jesus, and reports of an empty tomb. After hearing them out patiently, we are told Jesus then "opened their minds to understand the Scriptures". He explained from the Scriptures how everything was according to Gods plan. As they were listening to God's word their hearts were filled with joy, and later they recalled, "Were not our hearts burning within us while he was talking to us on the road, while he was opening the Scriptures to us?" (Lk 24:32). We can take up the Scriptures at any moment of need and ask the Holy Spirit to bring the word of God to speak into the anxieties, questions, troubles, struggles, and disappointments in our lives.

When we take up the Bible to read it we can joyfully expect that the Holy Spirit will use the word to speak to us. Bible reading should not just be a routine activity. We can liken it to opening a much-awaited letter from a close friend. In this case the author is the Lord himself. You experience it as something valuable in your hands and you want to open it as quickly as possible. We read it repeatedly, savouring every word written. The more we read it the more we cherish the word written and the more joyful we become. When reading the Bible our hearts should be alert and attentive to his voice. We wait with love and deep faith for God to speak to us. The attitude is like Samuel who was taught by Eli to respond, "Speak, Lord, for your servant is listening" (1 Sam 3:10). When God speaks to us through the word we will know it because the Holy Spirit will stir our hearts. We will have a moment of illumination from the Spirit, and we will feel that this word is just for me, giving me the solace I need at this moment, or the challenge I need to face my life-situation or some other message which I know is God's word for me right now.

When we read the Scriptures in the Spirit we not only need to be *expectant about hearing* God speak to us, and *be listening attentively* to the word being revealed, but we also will need to be *ready to obey* the voice of God. In James it says, "Be doers of the word, and not just hearers deceiving yourselves" (James 1:22). Mary, our Mother, was a wonderful example of this. When the word of God came to her, she responded, "Here I am, the servant of the Lord; let it be done to me according to your word" (Lk 1:38). Like Mary we must build our lives around the word of God, and do whatever the Spirit shows us is God's word for us. Jesus says, "It is not those who say 'Lord, Lord' who will gain the kingdom of heaven, but those who do the will of my father in heaven" (Mt 7:21ff). If we are not obedient to the word of God, it is like building our house on sand. When the wind and rains come it will fall because it is on poor foundations. The one who obeys God's word builds on rock and will not be shaken when troubles come.

5
PURIFYING FIRE

God is light; there is no darkness in him at all (1 Jn 1:5).

In a previous chapter we saw how the Holy Spirit acts as the fire of God's love poured out for us. Our God is a "consuming fire". His fire does not burn us up and obliterate us. Rather his burning love purifies us of all sin. God is Holy. He gives us the *Holy* Spirit. His purpose is to make us holy. The Lord says: "Be holy, for I am holy" (1 Pet 1:15). To be holy is not to become sanctimonious and excessively pious by multiplying devotions for their own sake. Nor does it necessarily mean becoming a monk or religious. It simply means being "set apart" for God by being formed into the likeness of Jesus, who is the Holy One of God. This is the work of the Spirit. St Paul says that all of us who personally encounter the glory of God shining on the face of Jesus "are being transformed into his likeness from one degree of glory to another; for this comes from the Lord, the Spirit" (2 Cor 3:18).

Burning out Impurities

The Lord is a jealous lover, who wants us for himself and will not rest until we truly belong to him. He alone is holy. To the degree that the Holy Spirit dwells within us, to that degree are we made holy, changed into his likeness. As God's holiness comes to dwell in us he will not tolerate any compromise or any dividedness of heart. He will strip away all evil and burn it up. Only those who reject every last trace of evil can live with this devouring fire of love. The one desire of their heart must be union with God. As Isaiah says, "Who among us can live with the devouring fire? Who among us can live with everlasting flames?" (Is 33:14). The answer is only those who change their heart and conform their lives totally to the will of God. The fire of God's love burns out all impurities, and makes us new.

The prophet Malachi uses the image of the purifying fire of God to call the people, especially the Levites, to a deeper level of holiness. Speaking of the "day of the Lord's coming", he says, "For he is like a refiner's fire and like a fuller's soap; he will sit as a refiner and purifier of silver, and he will purify the descendants of Levi and refine them like gold and silver, until they present offerings to the Lord in righteousness" (Mal 3:2-3). The Levites will not be able to offer sacrifices that are acceptable to the Lord until they themselves are made holy, until they are purified of their faults, like gold or silver is purified by fire. Only then will they be able to make a pure offering of themselves with a humble and contrite heart.

The prophet Isaiah experienced a theophany in the Temple when he saw angels singing, "Holy, holy, holy is the Lord of hosts; the whole earth is full of his glory." In the overwhelming presence of the holiness of God, Isaiah trembled with the utter conviction of his crass human nature which is so prone to sin, and felt full of remorse and a deep sense of unworthiness. He cried out, "Woe is me! I am lost, for I am a man of unclean lips, and live among a people of unclean lips; yet my eyes have seen the Lord of hosts!" (Is 6:5). Seeing Isaiah's openhearted remorse for his sinfulness, the Lord sent a seraph holding a live coal that had been taken from the altar with a pair of tongs. The seraph touched his mouth with it, saying, "Now that this has touched your lips, your guilt has departed and your sin is blotted out" (Is 6:7). Isaiah was purified by the divine fire of love. The holiness of God cannot abide with sin. Encountering God's holiness he was convicted of his sin and repented. The burning hot coal symbolizes the purifying fire. He was cleansed of his sin, and so able to stand in the presence of God, and was made ready for proclaiming the word of God.

Making Us Holy

The Holy Spirit dwells within us to sanctify us, to make us holy. He wants to shape us into the image of Christ. He is making us perfect as our heavenly Father is perfect. It is God's work within us. We are to cooperate fully with his activity by making a total "yes" to his refining work. Without the Spirit's action we remain stubborn and resistant. The sequence on Pentecost Sunday invokes the Spirit to bring conversion:

> *If thou take thy grace away,*
> *Nothing pure in man will stay;*
> *All his good is turned to ill*
> *Bend the stubborn heart and will*
> *Melt the frozen, warm the chill.*

In the first letter of John we are encouraged to think of the love that the Father has lavished on us by letting us be called children of God. For that is our identity (1 Jn 3:1). Yet even though we have been bestowed with such dignity, we still find sin within us. John is adamant that any sin within us is incompatible with being a child of God. God intends to make us like him, and eventually to have us with him forever in heaven, when we will see him as he really is. "All who have this hope in him purify themselves, just as he is pure" (1 Jn 3:3). In other words we can't settle for a certain degree of conversion. Although we belong to the Lord, we do not belong to him totally. To live a holy life is to be holy just as God is holy, but to live a sinful life is to belong to the devil (1 Jn 3:7-8). We must let God's work go more deeply into us, purifying us with his burning love. If we do not undergo this purgation here on earth we will surely need to go through purification in Purgatory after death.

Call to Repentance

The purifying work of the Spirit in our lives aims to eliminate sin from our hearts. For God this is an easy task, but for us who must cooperate with his work it is quite complicated. Firstly, the Spirit convinces us of the sinfulness that is present in our lives. Here the pang of conscience is a great blessing. While the Holy Spirit comes to comfort the afflicted, he comes to afflict the comfortable. In our complacency we can have "made a bed" for sinful patterns that need to be uprooted and overcome in our lives. The light of the Spirit within the heart helps us identify these sinful trends that may have been hidden from us. The Spirit shows us how devious our hearts are. We are convicted of deep levels of perversity, "sicknesses of the heart", deeply ingrained in us due to our fallen human condition. The so-called "capital" sins are a useful list from the spiritual tradition of the most notorious of these basic human flaws: gluttony, lust, greed, envy, anger, vanity and pride.[30] Fundamental to all of these primal disorders in the human heart is selfishness and pride, a refusal to give glory to God.

The Holy Spirit arouses the conscience to a state of remorse, an interior affliction of guilt, which in itself is a call to repentance. This in no way means unhealthy self-condemnation. Whipping ourselves with heavy doses of self-accusation and recrimination does not lead to repentance but despair. This self-centred toxic guilt drags us down into a pit of self-pity. We need to distinguish between healthy guilt and the sort of guilt that is driven by feelings of hopelessness. There is no condemnation in the heart of God. Yet a true conscience under the action of the Spirit will bring our thoughts and actions under judgment, not to feed any psychological low self-esteem or self-hate, but to call us to change, and to give us the power to change. When we experience genuine remorse we may well see for the first time how some of our thoughts and actions have been ugly, loathsome and despicable. But we will not find an interior "accuser", or "grand inquisitor", judging *our person* as ugly, loathsome and despicable. Rather, we will find the whisper of the Spirit of love, persuading us that our inner dignity is not being served by these rogue thoughts and actions. Hence we ought to be rid of them, and find a new way to live. In convicting us of sin the Holy Spirit is always intent on convincing us that we have a future full of hope.

Honesty before God

What can defeat us is our own inherent dishonesty. We have a tendency to cover up our sin rather than to face its reality and own it. The counter movement in the heart which is fed by the evil spirit seeks to deceive us that things are not going too badly. The Holy Spirit wants to "blow our cover" and have us candidly admit something is wrong. The Holy Spirit of truth works on us to face the truth and to stand in truth before ourselves, others and God. A parable can help us understand this.

Jimmy and his sister Annie loved to spend their holidays at Grandma's house in the country. They gladly shared doing the house work for Grandma since most of the day was spent having fun in the little farm which still had quite a range of animals. Anyway one day Jimmy decided to make a "shanghai", a sort of sling-shot that could catapult stones long distances. He had been trying out his new invention down by the river. But he had little success. Coming home to the farm house he saw one of Grandma's ducks not far away. A perfect target. He lined up his shot, and much to his delight he hit the duck in the head, and it fell down dead. However, the excitement of the moment turned sour in Jimmy very quickly, since he knew Grandma would not be happy about losing her duck. Standing over the dead duck he began to think that unless he did something he may end up a "dead duck" himself! No one was watching so he quickly dug a hole, threw the dead duck into it, and covered it over. Problem solved! He ambled into the house whistling as if nothing had happened. That night at washing up time Annie declared she won't be washing up anymore. Jimmy protested. But Annie informed him that she saw what happened out in the garden earlier, and surely Grandma would not want to know about it. So Jimmy was silenced and he did the washing up by himself. And now every time a chore was due, Annie let him know she would not be participating. There was no way out for Jimmy. He had to hide what he had done from Grandma. So very sad and burdened he continued labouring under the chores by himself. After a week of this he had had enough. "I am going to tell Grandma," he told himself, "At least I will be free of this burden." Sheepishly he approached Grandma in the kitchen. "Grandma, do you remember your duck?" "Yes", said Grandma. "Well, I was … well I shot your duck." To his great surprise Grandma replied, "Jimmy I know. I saw you do it from the upstairs window. I have been waiting for you to confess to me so I could forgive you."

King David's Cover-up

A biblical example of the same principle is found with David, King of Israel (2 Sam 11:1-12:7). David had lusted over Uriah the Hittite's wife, Bathsheba, when he saw her bathing in the house next door. Uriah was in David's army which was at war under the command of Joab. Since he was the King, David could have what he wanted. He called Bathsheba to his house, and slept with her. Some time later to his great dismay Bethsheba sent him a message that she was with child. David quickly moves into "cover up" mode. He recalls Uriah from the battle and tries various ruses to have Uriah go down to sleep with his wife. But Uriah was a man of honour. He did not want to have the comfort that his mates in the battlefield could not have. He slept at the palace and did not go to his wife. David then sent Uriah back to the battle with a sealed message for the eyes of Joab alone. He ordered Joab to post Uriah in the thick of the battle and to withdraw support so that Uriah would be killed. And that is what happened. Problem solved! At the appropriate time David could take Bethsheba as his wife.

But God sees everything, and the Lord was not pleased with David. The Lord sent the prophet Nathan to David, who told David a sad story of injustice. There were two men in a town, one rich and one poor. The rich man had plenty of sheep in abundance. The poor man had just a little lamb, which was a pet for him, and was "like a daughter to him". When a traveller came to town the rich man refused to provide from his own flock, but took the poor man's lamb and prepared it for his guest.

When David heard this story he was filled with righteous anger. "As the Lord lives, the man who did this deserves to die!" Nathan said to David, *"You are the man!"*

David now was confronted with the truth of his sin. To his great merit he was filled with remorse, and repented. Tradition tells us that the powerful penitential psalm 51 arose from his afflicted heart. The Holy Spirit will convict us of things we have tried to cover up. We will hear within us, "You are the one!" The gracious gift of the Spirit is to convince us of our sin, and bring us to genuine repentance.

A Humble and Contrite Heart

God is all powerful. He can do all things. However, he cannot bring us to repentance without our cooperation. He will knock on the door of the heart, but we are the ones who have the key to open the door. His Spirit will persuade and confront us, but we must allow ourselves to receive the gift of compunction, by which we weep for our sins. It is a grace, but it must be received freely by us. St Simeon the New Theologian writes:

> Even if one has a heart harder than bronze or iron or diamond, as soon as compunction enters, it becomes soft as wax. Compunction is the divine fire that melts mountains and rocks, that sweetly softens every hardness, that everywhere changes and totally transforms the souls that welcome it into a paradise ... all of that is brought about by the divine fire of compunction, along with tears, or let us rather say, by means of tears.[31]

The only sacrifice acceptable to God is that of a "humble and contrite heart" (Ps 51:19). There is where he wants to dwell. He who is Lord of the universe, and can freely dwell wherever he likes, is "drawn to the man of humbled and contrite heart, who trembles at his word" (Is 66:2). The Spirit's purpose in giving us the grace of a remorseful conscience, tears of compunction, honesty before God, and confession of our sins, has the purpose of granting a "new heart and a new spirit". The Psalmist prays, "A pure heart create for me, O God; put a steadfast spirit within me. Do not cast me away from your presence nor deprive me of your Holy Spirit" (Ps 51:12-13). The cry is for the Holy Spirit to live within the heart, because the Holy Spirit will bring purity.

> I shall pour clean water over you and you shall be cleansed. A new heart I will give you, and a new spirit I will put within

you; and I will remove from your body the heart of flesh. I will put my Spirit within you ... (Ez 36:25-26).

When we are moved by the Spirit to confess our sins we will do so with honesty, neither exaggerating our fault, nor blaming others for our sin. We will not be making excuses or rationalizing our defects. Rather we will be straightforward and transparent before the Lord.

The Holy Spirit and Forgiveness of Sins

The Sacrament of Reconciliation brings great joy to those who approach it with humility. The words of absolution are quite telling: "God the Father of mercies through the death and resurrection of his Son has reconciled us to himself and sent the Holy Spirit upon us for the forgiveness of sins." So the Holy Spirit who inspires repentance and confession, also brings remission of sins. St Basil says, "Purification from sin comes in the grace of the Holy Spirit."[32] On the Cross Jesus offered the one single sacrifice for the remission of sins which was all sufficient for our redemption. His blood was shed to wash away our sins (1 Jn 1:7; Rev 1:5). In the Sacrament of Reconciliation the Holy Spirit through the absolution of the priest applies the remission of sins won for us by Jesus to our life. When the Risen Jesus breathed the Holy Spirit upon the apostles and gave them the power to forgive sins, this was not only a bestowal of ecclesiastical authority. More than that, Jesus was giving the Spirit who actually forgives sins. He was giving the Church a real power, a power intrinsic to its being Church – the power of the Holy Spirit to bring forgiveness of sins. St Augustine stated simply, "The love that is poured into our hearts by the Holy Spirit is its very self the forgiveness of sins."[33] Sometimes we are inclined to think that there are two movements; firstly, Jesus forgives sins, and then the Holy Spirit is given to bring new life. That is not entirely accurate. The whole process of conversion is redolent with the Holy Spirit. The Holy Spirit convinces us of sin, the Holy Spirit inspires repentance of heart, the Holy Spirit opens the heart to confession, and the Holy Spirit bestows forgiveness of sin through the agency of the priest. Then the Holy Spirit fills us with new life, and recreating power for on-going personal transformation.

Changed from Within

After being initially confused by Jehovah's Witnesses, Joe, a sensitive 18-year-old, was blessed to meet a Christian couple who gave him books to read which awakened in him a hunger for the Holy Spirit. While sitting in an armchair, reading one of the books, he felt welling up within him the desire for God. He fell to his knees before the chair, and right there and then made a prayer of surrender to the Lord. He was touched by a profound experience of being loved and being accepted. But at the same time he felt such a rotten sinner. Like Peter in the boat after the miraculous catch of fish, he was saying, "Leave me Lord I am a sinful man." But what he felt radiating from the heart of God was infinite mercy. This gave him hope.

Not long after this experience, while Joe was looking for some tapes in a Catholic book shop, he was invited to a prayer group. From there he found out about a youth camp being organized for young adults. He went with hunger in his heart. There he heard the simple proclamation of the Good News of the death and resurrection of Jesus. He discovered that Jesus frees us from sin. He desperately wanted this liberation. But he was terrified of going to the Sacrament of Reconciliation, feeling deeply shameful for the patterns of sin that had kept him in bondage. While gazing upon the face of Jesus crucified, he was overwhelmed by the love shown for him. He found himself praying to Jesus, "If you got up and went to Calvary for me, I will get up and go to confession for you." The moment of confession was like being the prodigal son, embraced by the Father's love, a tangible experience of being unburdened and set free. Joe received a new outpouring of the Holy Spirit, and the gift of tongues began to flow, which became a beautiful way for him to be built up in prayer and to have courage to face his fears. He says, "I knew now I had something far beyond me dwelling within me. I could draw on this inner resource at any time – the Holy Spirit. The interior presence of the Spirit was like a wellspring in the heart from which I could draw, an assurance of God's accompaniment."

Some months later at a week-long school of discipleship Joe was convicted further of his sinfulness, and again overwhelmed by the mercy of God. But this time as he waited in line to confess to a priest he felt the immense transforming power of the Spirit, who was claiming him in love. As he felt himself drawn more and more into the purifying love of God, a sovereign and deep healing was happening. He says it was like having intensive heart surgery, as if a divine scalpel went to work deep within him. He was set free. Joe admits, of course, that his purification is an on-going work of transformation, which continues throughout life. But he is sure that now he is not alone in the journey, no longer having to make it happen by himself. The Holy Spirit, the power of God Most High, is within him, and that makes the difference.

6
POWER TO CHANGE

For anyone who is in Christ Jesus there is a new creation; the old creation has gone and the new one is here (2 Cor 5:17).

Overcoming the Flesh

The sanctifying work of the Holy Spirit incites a deep struggle within the human heart. An opposing force within us, which St Paul calls the "flesh", resists the Holy Spirit's activity. An intense battle ensues. The Holy Spirit comes to conquer the power of the flesh. But for this to happen we need to cooperate with the Spirit's activity. The selfish drives and passions within us are deeply ingrained in our make-up. This drive towards sin, which tradition has called "concupiscence", is in us as a result of original sin. Even though the sacrament of Baptism washes us clean of original sin, the dynamic force of the "flesh", or "concupiscence", remains and if left unchecked will destroy us.

The critical question for each of us is: "What will be the governing principle of my life, the flesh or the Spirit?" Or put another way: "Will I become a genuinely spiritual person, one who is moved by the Spirit, led by the Spirit, living under the direction and control of the Spirit; or will I be a carnal person governed by the selfish drives of the flesh?" The flesh is self-centred, seeking self-gratification and self-indulgence. It drives us towards exalting ourselves before others, craving their attention and finding ways for self-promotion. It works to convince us we should avoid serving others in a sacrificial way; rather we should ensure our comfort and our own convenience. It refuses to come under any authority, demanding always to have its own way. St Paul himself admitted to this interior struggle:

> I do not understand my own actions. For I do not do what I want, but I do the very thing I hate … For I know that nothing good dwells within me, that is, in my flesh. I can will what is right but I cannot do it (Rom 7:15-19).

Paul goes on to exclaim, "Who will rescue me from this body of death? Thanks be to God through Jesus Christ our Lord!" Yes, we are rescued through what Jesus Christ did on the Cross for our sake. And it is the role of the Holy Spirit to make what happened on the Cross subjectively operative in our lives. How is the battle to be won? We must surrender our lives to the action of the Holy Spirit. The Holy Spirit will crucify the flesh, bringing the saving power of the Cross against it, and breaking its power in our lives. When we come under the ownership of the Holy Spirit God restores us to fullness of life.

Faith in the Cross of Jesus

We cannot break the power of the flesh by just "trying to be good" or "gritting our teeth" and working hard on our spiritual improvement. This attitude is akin to what Paul calls trying to live by the law. The law shows us where we are failing, but does not give us the power to change. By our will-power alone it is impossible to win the battle. Writing of the victory he had won, Paul says, "I am no longer trying for perfection that comes from the law, but rather that which comes through faith in Christ" (Phil 3:9). Even though we may try to keep all the rules and live by the commandments, if we are doing it in our own strength we are destined for failure and disappointment. We must humbly admit our helplessness to become holy, and surrender to the power of the Holy Spirit. We do this by putting our faith in what Jesus has done on the Cross to rescue us from the power of sin, and by calling on the Holy Spirit to apply this new power to our lives. By the work of the Holy Spirit within us we can stop striving to be perfect on our own terms, and instead begin to rely on the grace of God. The Holy Spirit, through the power of the Cross of Jesus, will give us authority over our fleshy inclinations.

The work of the Spirit overcoming the power of the flesh is painful and many refuse to go through the agony of it all. It is nothing less than crucifixion. St Paul said, "I have been crucified with Christ; and it is no longer I who live, but it is Christ who lives in me" (Gal 2:19-20). The work of the Spirit hurts, because we must change. We have to put to death the works of the flesh. St Paul warns, "If you live according to the flesh, you will die; but if by the Spirit you put to death the deeds of the body, you will live" (Rom 8:13). The self-denial and self-discipline involved is far more challenging than any "boot camp" or extreme sport that one may undergo for adventurous kicks. The Holy Spirit is relentless in his loving desire to claim us as his own. When we allow this ownership to take place, we actually then become who we are fully meant to be. However, the only way to attain genuine freedom, having authority over our passions and desires, is through the Cross. As St Paul says, "Those who belong to Christ Jesus have crucified the flesh with its passions and desires" (Gal 5:24).

Breaking Patterns of Sin

Even though we may be committed Christians we can still be dogged by old patterns of sin that resurface periodically. We wonder whether we can ever be free of them. These old habits of sin can be ingrained in our personality. We can feel they are so much part of us that we may not even *want* to be delivered from them. They are the grooves of the old self that we find ourselves falling back into again and again. We can feel like our life is an old record playing the same sorrowful song over and over again. We can find ourselves embarrassed to confess yet again the same disordered habits and tendencies. Is there any way out?

There is no trite answer to the question. Our growth in the Spirit has many stops and starts, many failures and times of repentance. We fall and we pick ourselves up again. No one's journey is plain sailing without crises of one kind or another. We all have our areas of weakness, and God's mercy, ministered especially in the Sacrament of Reconciliation, has no bounds. We can certainly be helped by pastoral counseling, being vulnerable and accountable with a mentor, and if necessary psychological counseling and therapy. The Holy Spirit can be working through all of these mediums. Nevertheless, it is important not to lose sight of the *primary* way the Spirit comes to help us and set us free. When the Holy Spirit is released more fully within us, we find a *new power* to break these patterns of sin. This is a power and energy the world knows nothing about. As good as the social sciences are for our growth, they do not draw directly upon this power. This is the power of the Cross of Jesus, his death and resurrection, which has unleashed new energy into the universe to be drawn upon for human living. Not enough Christians are fully convinced of this power.

Victory Over Sin

No longer do we have to walk through life feeling defeated by patterns of sin, and threatened by forces within us and outside of us that seem to hold us back. The Good News of the death and resurrection of Jesus gives us new hope. When Jesus hung on the cross for our sake he put to death the sin of humankind. When the Father raised Jesus from the dead he sealed this victory. The Father together with Jesus at his right hand, sent the Holy Spirit to make of us a new creation.

In Ephesians Paul prays that "you may be strengthened in your inner being by the *power* of his Holy Spirit" and then at the end of the prayer cries, "Glory be to him whose *power* within us can do infinitely more than we can ask or imagine" (Eph 3:20).

This should give us enormous confidence in the fight against sin. We have the victory of Jesus already applied to our lives by the Holy Spirit in Baptism. Paul tells us that when we were baptized we were joined with Jesus in his death. It is as if we went into the tomb with him. But Jesus was raised from the tomb by the Father in the power of the Holy Spirit. So in Baptism we too were joined with Jesus in his resurrection. Paul says, "We know that our old self was crucified with him so that the body of sin might be destroyed, and we might no longer be enslaved to sin" (Rom 6:6). What is this "body of sin"? Could it not be the accumulated sin of our lives which has settled in our hearts like the growth of a stalagmite in a limestone cave, which grows from the sediment of years of erosion?[34] This "body of sin" is destroyed! What Good News! Paul goes on to say, "When Christ died, he died once for all, to sin, so his life now is life with God; and in that way, you too must consider yourselves to be dead to sin but alive for God in Christ Jesus" (Rom 6:11). He is proclaiming with great authority that sin does not have to dominate our lives any more. Such is the mercy of our God!

Resurrection Power

Paul was no doubt familiar with the Genesis account of the first creation. The breath of God, the "Ruah", or Spirit, hovered over the chaos, bringing order and new life. The same Spirit hovered over the dead body of Jesus, and the Father raised him from the dead to be the "first fruits" of the *new* creation. This Holy Spirit now lives in us. We have unlimited power to be able to change. Paul says, "If the

Spirit of him who raised Jesus from the dead dwells in you, he who raised Christ from the dead will give life to your mortal bodies also through his Spirit that dwells in you" (Rom 8:11). When Paul speaks of giving "life to your mortal bodies" he is not only referring to the resurrection of the body on the last day. He means our historical existence right now. Christ is risen in our hearts by the Spirit given to us, and this is our hope. This resurrection power gives us the energy to live as a new creation. As he says elsewhere, "So if anyone is in Christ, there is a new creation: everything old has passed away; see, everything has become new!" (2 Cor 5:17).

How can the power of the cross and resurrection of Jesus, given to us in the Spirit, take effect in our lives? In faith we must appropriate the grace of our Baptism. We must give our personal "yes" to what has been done by Christ. We must repent of our sin, acknowledge Jesus as the Saviour and Lord of our lives. We must surrender to the power of the Holy Spirit. We must consciously take hold of the grace of our Baptism. Paul is constantly reminding his communities that they have already received all they need for their salvation and their sanctification. He reminds them, "When the goodness and loving kindness of our Saviour appeared, he saved us, not because of any works of righteousness we had done, but according to his mercy, through the water of rebirth and the renewal by the Holy Spirit" (Titus 3:5). Because this grace has already been given us, which we have not deserved, we must no longer cling to our old ways of thinking and acting. We must change our lives, drawing upon the power given to us in Christ: "You must give up your old way of life; you must put aside your old self, which gets corrupted by following illusory desires. Your mind must be renewed by a spiritual revolution, so that you can put on the new self that has been created in God's way, in the goodness and holiness of the truth" (Eph 4:22-24).

Renewing the Mind

Our sanctification depends on having a transformed mind. This is the work of the Holy Spirit. Appealing to us to make our lives as a "living sacrifice, holy and acceptable to God", St Paul urges, "do not be conformed to this world, but be transformed by the renewing of your minds, so that you may discern what is the will of God – what is good and acceptable and perfect" (Rom 12:1). The renewal of the mind by the action of the Holy Spirit sets us free from being captive to a worldly mind-set, and brings us under God's authority. We are not to be conformed to the thinking of "the world". By this Paul means the whole set of ideals, values, desires and attitudes which make up a whole "world-view" that is commonly held in the prevailing culture. If our minds are in allegiance to this way of thinking they are blocked from having allegiance to the Kingdom of God. The "world" is an ideal in the minds of people that suggests a heart captive to a whole way of life that shuts out the Good News of Jesus Christ. In "worldly thinking" money is paramount, instant sexual gratification is dominant, ambition, honour and status are hotly pursued, unbridled pleasure is the game, things are more important than persons, and the value of human life is relative. The Holy Spirit of truth shows us how shallow the "world" is and illuminates the mind with the truth. As John wrote,

> Do not love the world or the things of the world. The love of the Father is not in those who love the world; for all that is in the world – the desire of the flesh, the desire of the eyes, the pride in riches – comes not from the Father but from the world. And the world and its desires are passing away, but those who do the will of God live forever (1 Jn 2:15-15).

God is a jealous lover and he wants us for his own. The Holy Spirit comes to enliven our inner self, attracting us towards the love of God and doing his will. His loving approach seeks to win us for God. He reveals to us how everything that may have a hold on our heart is passing. In the end, only possession of God matters. All our self-centred efforts towards happiness are to no avail. Only God suffices. The Spirit reveals to us the truth of what Jesus has done on the Cross for us, and shows us the immensity of his love for us. The Spirit brings to us the power of the resurrected Christ and gives us the guarantee that the resurrection power of Christ dwells within us. He discloses to us the falsity of the ways of the world, and shows us clearly the choice that we must make. As James says, "Do you not know that friendship with the world is enmity with God?" (James 4:4). The battle is in our minds and wills. The Holy Spirit comes to enlighten the darkened mind and to bend the stubborn will. St Paul encourages the Ephesians:

> Now this I affirm and insist on in the Lord: you must no longer live as the pagans live, in the futility of their minds. They are darkened in their understanding, alienated from the life of God because of their ignorance and hardness of heart (Eph 4:17-18).

Paul speaks about the empty futility of the minds of people who are living according to the thinking of the world. They have no real reason to live, no direction or purpose, without meaning and without hope. This sort of mind is "darkened" without any real perception of God. People enslaved in this way are shut out from the fullness of life offered in Jesus. Paul goes on to say, "They have lost all sensitivity and have abandoned themselves to licentiousness, greedy to practise every kind of impurity. *That is not the way you learned Christ!*" (Eph 4:19-20). What a wonderful phrase! We are the ones who are meant to "learn Christ". Christ is our model, we are to be conformed to him. We live according to his attitudes, his ideals, his values, his vision of life.

Abiding in Christ

Modelling ourselves on Christ is not an extrinsic exercise of just looking at Jesus as we find him in the gospels and trying to imitate him. It is only effective if we are filled with the Holy Spirit whose indwelling presence makes us live "in Christ". Paul says, "Let the same mind be in you that was in Christ Jesus" (Phil 2:5). This happens as we become more one with Christ by the indwelling, and transformative activity of the Holy Spirit. John's Gospel expresses it poignantly when Jesus says,

> Abide in me as I abide in you. Just as the branch cannot bear fruit by itself unless it abides in the vine, neither can you unless you abide in me. I am the vine, you are the branches. Those who abide in me and I in them bear much fruit, because apart from me you can do nothing (Jn 15:4-5).

We abide in Christ and he in us through the indwelling of the Holy Spirit. As Christ is the vine and we the branches the Holy Spirit could well be the sap flowing through the vine which keeps the branches alive. Unless we cooperate with the work of the Spirit to change our minds so that we think like Christ, our lives will be driven by the endless turmoil of emotions and the tyranny of circumstances, dictated by fate. Paul says:

> For those who live according to the flesh set their minds on the things of the flesh, but those who live according to the Spirit set their minds on the things of the Spirit. To set the mind on the flesh is death, but to set the mind on the Spirit is life and peace. For this reason the mind that is set on the flesh is hostile to God; it does not submit to God's law – indeed it cannot, and those who are in the flesh cannot please God (Rom 8:5-8).

This is in stark contrast to someone who is alive in the Spirit and has a transformed mind. We need to develop an active mind, rather than mindlessly absorbing the values and attitudes of the world. We should be vigilant and alert, guarding our minds; so that every thought becomes captive in obedience to Christ Jesus (2 Cor 10:5). We need to free the mind of all encumbrances and keep the focus on the truth that sets us free. In the first letter of Peter we find a call to action, "Gird up your minds, be sober, set your hope fully upon the grace that is coming to you at the revelation of Jesus Christ" (1 Pet 1:13). What does it mean to "gird up your minds"? The original Greek text is literally, "gird up the loins of your mind". The image evoked here is of the long, flowing robes common in many cultures in the Near East. If they want to move fast they have to hoist up their robes and tuck them under their belts to be ready for action. We are to have active minds, not just absorbing any idea or image presented. It is a call to vigilance, to be alert to the false and illusory messages of the world often presented in attractive ways by television, the secular press and the media generally. What we feed the mind is vitally important for our spiritual growth. Paul urges us,

> Whatever is true, whatever is honourable, whatever is just, whatever is pure, whatever is pleasing, whatever is commendable, if there is any excellence and if there is anything worthy of praise, think about these things ... and the God of peace will be with you (Phil 4:8-9).

Feeding Our Minds

The world's agenda brings deception and confusion to the mind. The Holy Spirit within us brings clarity and light. The Holy Spirit will especially use the word of God to nourish our minds and purify our hearts. We need to feed our minds daily with the sacred word from Scripture, which gives us a new energy and a new way of thinking according to Gods way of thinking. His word will prune us and help us to grow (Jn 15:1). We make God's word the measure of our lives. It becomes the standard by which we judge our behaviour. The word of God is "alive and active; it cuts like any double-edged sword but more finely … it can judge the secret emotions and thoughts" (Heb 4:12). When we are truly vigilant in our minds we can spot quickly the deceptive thought, we can discern the sinful or disordered images or memories that arise within us, and we can put them to death by dashing them against the cross of Jesus.

One of the early fathers, John Cassian, offers an image for this vigilance of heart.[35] He describes the continual flow of thoughts through the mind as a millstone spinning around under the power of a waterfall. As long as the water is running there is a lot of activity. Yet the miller can decide what is going to be ground by the stone. He can grind wheat, barley or darnel, and the stone will work on whatever he chooses. In other words while we can't stop the flow of thoughts in the mind, we can take charge over what comes into it. If we fill our minds with bad grain in the morning it will grind away with that content all day long. On the other hand, if we put into our minds in the morning good clean grain, good thoughts, good words, then it will grind away with these throughout the day. Rather than put into the mind the latest thoughts of a popular radio announcer we would do well to put God's word into our minds at the beginning of the day, and allow the Spirit to cleanse our minds with this word throughout the day. If we are constantly turning over the word of God in our hearts they will be oriented towards God, and not governed by worldly thinking.

Scrutiny of the Heart

Attaining a true peace of mind, through being sober and watchful about what is running through it, can be assisted by a regular scrutiny of our hearts; being in touch with what has been running within them in the course of the day just passed. Diadochos of Photike, one of the Eastern Fathers, says that a purified mind is like a tranquil sea:

> Those pursuing the spiritual way must always keep the mind free from agitation in order that the intellect, as it discriminates among the thoughts that pass through the mind, may store in the treasuries of its memory those thoughts which are good and have been sent by God, while casting out those which are evil and come from the devil.
>
> When the sea is calm, fishermen can scan its depths and therefore hardly any creature moving in the water escapes their notice. But when the sea is disturbed by the winds, it hides beneath its turbid and agitated waves what it was happy to reveal when it was smiling and calm; and then the fishermen's skill and cunning prove to be in vain.[36]

When we are driven by the flesh and enamored with the world, the soul is agitated. Anxiety and disturbance of heart kill the soul. The mind is running all the time, driven by destructive pursuits, and unable to know what is really happening in the depths of the heart. There is little vigilance. Like the apostles in the Garden of Gethsemane we have fallen asleep, overcome by the burden of the world, seduced by Satan into a state of torpor. In Mark's gospel Jesus in the Garden says to the apostles, "The spirit is willing, but the flesh is weak" (Mk 14:38). For Mark *to sleep* has profound significance; it means to succumb to the power of Satan through giving in to the flesh, to be in a stupor, and hence not to know what is really going on. At the time of testing the apostles fail to stay awake. This is in sharp contrast to Jesus, who at the time of his greatest testing has his mind fixed on the Father, and doing the Father's will. This is the mind of Christ which we want to have. Diadochus reminds us that the light of the Holy Spirit shines in the mind that is submitted to Christ:

> Only the Holy Spirit can purify the intellect ... In every way, therefore, and especially through peace of soul, we must make ourselves a dwelling-place for the Holy Spirit. Then we shall have the lamp of spiritual knowledge burning always within us, and when it is shining constantly in the inner shrine of the soul, not only will the intellect perceive all the dark and bitter attacks of the demons, but these attacks will be greatly weakened when exposed for what they are by that glorious and holy light.[37]

Becoming a New Creation

In Baptism we are "born again" in the Spirit. Jesus said to Nicodemus, "Very truly, I tell you, no one can enter the Kingdom of God without being born of water and the Spirit" (Jn 3:5). Through our baptism we become children of God and heirs to the Kingdom of God. St Paul says, "For all who are led by the Spirit of God are children of God. For you did not receive a spirit of slavery to fall back into fear, but you have received a spirit of adoption. When we cry 'Abba! Father!', it is that very Spirit bearing witness with our spirit that we are children of God, and if children, then heirs, heirs of God and joint heirs with Christ" (Rom 8:14-17).

When we become aware of the truth of our Baptism we realize that we have been reborn in the Spirit. There is only one Son of God, but by the Spirit's adoption of us we have become sons and daughters *in the Son*. This is our deepest identity, and the source of our most profound dignity. We are heirs to all the promises of the Kingdom of

God. We have been set free from the slavery of the old self, which was constantly falling back into sin; and now we have been made new by the action of the Spirit, making it possible for us to live in virtue. The Holy Spirit has begun a work of refashioning us in the image of God. While God originally created us in his image and likeness, this reality has been disfigured by sin. We need to be remade.

Through the rebelliousness of sin our human nature had been deeply wounded. Our human faculties of mind, will, imagination, memory and emotions no longer functioned according to their design. We were captive to the power of the flesh and the devil. Now through the gift of the Holy Spirit we are being remade. This has already happened in sacramental Baptism at the level of being, but now it needs outworking in our whole human make-up. Our original design had been wounded by sin. But now the grace of the Holy Spirit heals and restores us. It is a type of "image-restoration".

In popular parlance people talk about "reinventing" themselves. That sort of change is a comparatively superficial re-making by altering one's outward *persona* and appearance before others. Here we are talking about a much deeper restoration. When the Holy Spirit recreates us, the remaking is a change from inside to outside. We are being refashioned into the image of God. This recreating work of the Spirit is a project with which we must cooperate, allowing what has already been given in the depth of our being through Baptism to now become fruitful in the whole of our personality. Paul assures us, "So if anyone is in Christ, there is a new creation: everything old has passed away; see, everything has become new!" (2 Cor 5:17).

The recreating work of the Spirit is accomplished through growth in virtue. This means the Holy Spirit wants to change us into the very likeness of Jesus, to have his attitudes, his way of thinking, his way of acting. Virtues are qualities of the heart of a person which are formed under the action of the Spirit as we learn habitual ways of acting which are according to the mind of God. By developing in virtue we become more fully human, in imitation of Jesus, who was most perfectly human. As we cooperate with the recreating work of the Spirit virtues such as humility, practical love, obedience, prudence, justice, fortitude and temperance develop. We become more Christ-like. The more we surrender our lives to the redeeming action of Christ, under the action of the Spirit, the more we will be able to develop in our lives the heart attitudes, ways of thinking and dispositions that are truly according to the mind of Christ.

There is a choice before us. We can either succumb to the persuasion of the "old self", still being dictated to by selfish desire, or we can gain victory over ourselves by choosing to surrender to the Holy Spirit and live a new life in Christ. Only then does the real self emerge. We experience ourselves as a new creation. St Paul urges us to make this choice for a new life:

> You were taught to put away your former way of life, your old self, corrupt and deluded by its lusts, and to be renewed in the spirit of your minds and to clothe yourselves with the new self, created according to the likeness of God in true righteousness and holiness (Eph 4:22-24).

Cyprian of Carthage

The conversion of Cyprian of Carthage, North Africa, took place around 246AD when he was a middle-aged, sophisticated, and respected citizen of Carthage. Only two years after his baptism into the Christian faith he was elected to be Bishop of Carthage. His writings are revered as some of the most important in the history of the Church. His personal testimony of his Baptism shows how it was a very tangible experience of rebirth in the Spirit:

> I was myself so entangled and constrained by the very many errors of my former life that I could not believe it possible for me to escape from them, so much was I subservient to the faults which clung to me; and in despair of improvement I cherished these evils of mine as if they had been my dearest possessions.
>
> But when the stain of my earlier life had been washed away by the help of the water of birth, and light from above had poured down upon my heart, now cleansed and purified; when I had drunk the Spirit from heaven, and the second birth had restored me so as to make me a new man; then straightaway in a marvellous manner doubts began to be resolved, closed doors to open, dark places to grow light; what before had seemed difficult was now easy, what I had thought impossible was now capable of accomplishment.[38]

Cyprian went on to say that what had been "born of the flesh" and lived under the slavery of sin, was put to death. Now through the Spirit he knew he "belonged to God". This can only be explained by sheer gift from God. All our power for good is derived from God, for he is the source of our life and strength.

7
ENDOWED WITH CHARISMS

Each one of you has received a special grace, so, like good stewards responsible for all these different graces from God, put yourselves at the service of others (1 Pet 4:10).

What are Charisms?

So far our description of the life-changing power of the Holy Spirit has been primarily about the *sanctifying* work of the Spirit. But in addition to this work of personal transformation, making us holy, there is another more specifically *charismatic* activity of the Spirit. When people experience the spiritual awakening of the baptism in the Spirit, they begin to manifest spiritual gifts, called charisms. A charism is a gift given for the common good. St Paul gives a number of lists of charisms, but these lists are not meant to be exhaustive.[39] The Church has a broad vision for a variety of charisms, without determining a set number. To the Corinthians Paul says,

> To each is given the manifestation of the Spirit for the common good. To one is given through the Spirit the utterance of wisdom, and to another the utterance of knowledge according to the same Spirit, to another faith by the same Spirit, to another gifts of healing by the one Spirit, to another working of miracles, to another prophecy, to another the discernment of spirits, to another various kinds of tongues, to another the interpretation of tongues.

All these are activated by one and the same Spirit, who allots to each one individually just as the Spirit chooses" (1 Cor 12:7-11).

Charisms are not primarily given for the sanctification of the individual who receives them. Rather they are given for the service of others to build up the Church. It is possible for people to exercise even extraordinary charisms, while their personal lives still exhibit significant disorder. However, in that case the charism is not truly building up the Body of Christ, and it will in time dissipate and be lost. The point is that the presence of a charism is not of itself an indication of personal holiness. Nevertheless, the more we are endowed with charisms the more responsibility we have to pursue holiness, so the gifts will be exercised with integrity and responsibility.

Charisms, or spiritual gifts, differ from natural talents. They are "a manifestation of supernatural power".[40] Talents are inherent to our natural make-up, sometimes inherited or more often developed through the manner of our upbringing and education. They are certainly part of the gift of ourselves that, as followers of Jesus, we surrender to the Lord. Our talents can be used mightily for the Kingdom of God. But they are not charisms, which are given directly by the Holy Spirit. Talents come to us by natural birth, but a charism comes as a free and sovereign act of God, flowing from the grace of our Baptism. While a talent may be inherited, a charism cannot. However, it seems that sometimes a talent that we already possess provides a natural base for receiving a supernaturally empowered charism. For example, someone who has a natural singing voice may be gifted with the charism of music. By this supernatural gifting they become a channel of God's goodness to others through singing in a worship ministry for the praise of God. The more extraordinary the charism the less likely that it will be supported by a previously held talent. However, whether charisms are "extraordinary" (such as prophecy, healing, discernment of spirits) or quite "ordinary" (such as administration, service, hospitality, or mercy) they are all supernaturally empowered.

Charisms and the Seven gifts of the Spirit[41]

When celebrating the Sacrament of Confirmation, the bishop laid hands on us and prayed for the Holy Spirit to come upon us. His prayer asked God to bestow on us the seven "gifts of the Holy Spirit". These seven gifts are not the same as the charisms, even though some of them have similar names to charismatic gifts. The gifts of the Spirit prayed for at Confirmation are for our individual sanctification. They don't belong in the more charismatic sphere. These seven gifts (wisdom, understanding, counsel, fortitude, knowledge, piety and fear of the Lord) are based on a text from Isaiah 11:1-3. In the spiritual tradition they have been interpreted as enabling the interior heart to obey more easily and promptly the voice and impulse of the Spirit. They habitually dispose the person to the interior promptings of the Spirit. Under the direct action of the Spirit these gifts are means towards growth in sanctity. They are part of our inner transformation into becoming more Christ-like under the action of the Spirit. These gifts are *for us*. The charisms are different; they are *for others*. They are not focused on our inner growth, but focused outwardly, empowering us to love others and serve them in works of compassion and evangelization.

The irony in all this is that contemporary Scripture study has shown that the text in Isaiah used as the basis of the seven gifts of the Spirit was in fact referring to messianic *charisms*, rather than personal interior transformation.[42] But because the Church's theology had lost focus on the charisms, the text was interpreted to support the sanctifying work of the Spirit, rather that the charismatic manifestation of the Spirit. This does not annul the teaching of the seven gifts as handed down in the Tradition by countless spiritual writers and theologians. Rather, it alerts us to a gap that had existed for centuries in the Church's theology. The charismatic gifts were overlooked by the theologians and were only dealt with in hagiography, the stories of the lives of the saints. Why did this happen?

History of Charisms in the Church

In the apostolic Church, as witnessed by the New Testament, charisms were a normal and expected dimension of Christian communal life. In the Acts of the Apostles we can see a continuation of the charismatic ministry of Jesus. The Spirit conferred on Jesus the Messianic anointing, so that he could bring the Good News to the poor, release the captives, give sight to the blind, free the oppressed, heal the sick, and cast out demons (Lk 4:18-19). The early Church simply continued the ministry of Jesus in the power of the Spirit, manifesting the charisms of wisdom, knowledge, prophecy, healing, deliverance from demons, and many other gifts for this work of service and evangelization. As with the ministry of Jesus, the charisms were not private activities, not something just for the individual. They were part of the structure of the community. The early Church had apostolic authority, and an emerging sacramental order, but it was also thoroughly charismatic in expression.

It is not possible here to explore all the circumstances that led to a loss of the exercise of the charisms in the Church community. One of these factors was the false teaching of the Gnostics. Another was the rise of Montanism and the defection of a major figure such as Tertullian to that sect. Montanism was among other things an aberration of the gift of prophecy, since Montanists claimed that the Spirit was speaking exclusively through them, and not through Church authority.[43] Over time the charisms were seen to be esoteric and exotic, not intended for the normal activity of the Church. Gradually they disappeared from public view. However, some charisms persisted here and there for a time. Irenaeus writing around the year 180AD gives testimony to charisms still being alive. He testifies to "many brothers in the Church who have the prophetic charisms, who speak in many tongues, who reveal the secrets of men's hearts to their benefit, and who explain the mysteries of God".[44] Despite the sporadic use of the charisms by the faithful, gradually their use tended to become more associated with the clergy than the laity. Widespread use of the charisms disappeared. This was understandable in a way since, under the pressure of heresy, the pastors of the Church had to exercise their authority strongly. This tendency of "clericalization" was also aided by the prevailing theological perspective that gifts of the Spirit were more about personal holiness, and it was presumed that priests, monks and religious were the holy ones.

Charisms Restored

In this brief historical survey we must not assume that the charisms were lost to the life of the Church entirely. It would be more accurate to say they were lost to the *public* life of the Church but still manifest in the lives of individuals, especially the saints. Church history is full of charismatic preachers, evangelizers, prophets and teachers (doctors of the Church). Many of the saints had extraordinary gifts of healing, miracles, deliverance from demons, discernment of spirits, words of knowledge, and supernatural wisdom. When we take a broad sweep of history we can also see waves of charismatic awakenings, when the Spirit was poured out in new and tumultuous ways. The charisms were not lost to the life of the Church, but lost to its theology, and lost to its public life. They had been relegated to the private sphere of the individual, no longer being exercised for the common good, and no longer seen as essential to the life of the Church. They were expected only in the lives of clerics through ordination and in the extraordinarily holy lives of some monks, religious, and the occasional lay person.

Given this background we can maybe obtain a better appreciation of the renewal opened by the Second Vatican Council in the *Dogmatic Constitution on the Church*, when we read:

> It is not only through the sacraments and the ministries of the Church that the Holy Spirit makes holy the People, leads them and enriches them with his virtues. Allotting his gifts according as he wills (cf. 1 Cor 12:11), he also distributes special graces among the faithful of every rank. By these gifts he makes them fit and ready to undertake various tasks and offices for the renewal and building up of the Church, as it is written, "the manifestation of the Spirit is given to everyone for profit" (1 Cor 12:7). Whether these charisms be very remarkable or more simple and widely diffused, they are to be received with thanksgiving and consolation since they are fitting and useful for the needs of the Church.[45]

The Council makes clear that the charisms are distributed "among the faithful of every rank". All baptized Christians, who surrender to the grace of their Baptism, can expect to receive charisms of one kind or another, depending on the mysterious will of God. Some will exercise a charism once or twice and then no more. Others will exercise a charism occasionally. But what is most useful for the Church is when a charism is given on a permanent basis, so the one who receives it can be relied upon to exercise it whenever the opportunity arises and the charism is needed. Those who have experienced an adult conversion akin to being baptized in the Spirit can expect that the Spirit will give them at least one or more charisms, to be exercised in a long term manner, for the sake of the Church and its mission in the world.

Discerning Charisms

Since we can be sure that God is giving us charisms, we need to discern what these charisms are.[46] There are a few basic signs of a charism that we can expect to be consistently present over time. When you have a charism something far greater than anything you have to give passes through you and may even leave you quite astonished. There is an *effectiveness* that cannot be accounted for by your own natural abilities. If you have been given a charism of teaching then under your instruction people will be inspired to learn and excited to acquire knowledge. If you have the gift of hospitality you will find that people who are strangers will feel really at home with you, and when you reach out to them, they will feel welcome and find healing in opening their hearts to you. Another sign is that when you are exercising a charism you *feel energized*, satisfied and joyful. If you have been given a charism of preaching you will not feel that this ministry is a burden, but you will enjoy doing it, and will feel this is where you belong. Or if you have been given a charism of service you will delight in giving time to others in need and will quickly recognize problems of certain situations, and needs of others, and really want to make a difference by helping to solve these problem and meet these needs. The Lord does not give us charisms to make us feel miserable. The Lord knows what is best for us, and he will give us the gifts that will make us shine with his love.

Another sign that we have been given a charism is the response and affirmation of others. Sometimes we get direct feedback from people.

"I feel so much better after having shared with you my struggle," or "That word you spoke went straight to my heart." This can help confirm that the gift has been given. Sometimes indications from others are less direct, but still a sign of a charism. People may come to you to seek advice on difficult issues in life. (Is this an indication of a gift of wisdom?). People may just open up to you the worries of their lives, seeking a word of kindness. (Is this an indication of a gift of encouragement?). Often others recognize our gift in us before we do; they will seek us out for what the Lord is doing in us before we ourselves fully realize what is happening.

A final sign is that the exercise of the charism draws us more into intimacy with the Lord. While I made the case that charisms are independent of holiness, we can still expect that if we are exercising a divinely given gift that it will provide a way for us to be in communion with the Giver. God doesn't separate himself from his charisms as if they are some mechanical tool that he puts in our hands. As we use our charisms we are seeking to do so in a loving manner, according to the mind of God, and in a mysterious way we will find it brings us a sense of closeness to God as we are acting as an instrument in his hands.

Protecting Charisms

While the Church now has opened the window to the Holy Spirit in a new way, and welcomed enthusiastically the wide-spread exercise of spiritual gifts among faithful from all states of life, she still warns us to order the use of the gifts appropriately and not to misuse these gifts.[47] How can we make sure that the charisms that the Lord gives us will be used for the upbuilding of the Church and its mission? How can we avoid problems of presumption, competitiveness, division, self-aggrandisement, proprietary claims on the gifts, and many more aberrations that can occur. The Church encourages us to pray for the charisms and to use them confidently, but there is always a cautious note as well. It is possible for the charisms to become a threat to the unity of the Body of Christ and endanger our very soul. With every gift comes great responsibility; the larger the gift the greater the responsibility. How best can those who receive charisms exercise them with integrity and responsibility?

The answer is in personal holiness. While I have insisted that charisms are not given to us because of our personal holiness, at the same time we need to know that charisms will only flourish well in the fertile ground of holiness. In the spiritual tradition three habitual qualities of heart, that is three virtues, have been paramount in discerning holiness. They are practical love, humility and obedience.[48] If we are growing in these virtues then the charisms will be safe. Taking obedience first, we must insist on obedience to the authority of the Church. The Church is both institutional and charismatic. At times the charismatic feels hard done by the institution; and at times the institution feels hard done by the charismatic. Yet these two dimensions are "co-essential."[49] One cannot do without the other. The history of Catholic Charismatic Renewal is one of great blessing in this regard. From the beginning the leaders of the Renewal had a strong desire to remain in communion with the hierarchy. And by God's providence from very early in its history the Papal magisterium recognized the Renewal as "a chance for the Church and the world."[50]

This quality of obedience, which is so important for ordering the charisms, is more generally obedience to the will of God. This is the test of true discipleship. There is a text in Matthew's gospel which should make all charismatics shudder. After speaking about "good fruit" as a sign of the soundness of a tree, and if the tree does not bear good fruit it should be cut down, Jesus says, "You will know them by their fruits" (Mt 7:20). Ultimately the fruits of the Spirit in our lives will tell the story of authenticity, even in regard to the use of charisms. Jesus then goes on to speak of the "fruit" of obedience. "Not everyone who says to me 'Lord, Lord,' will enter the kingdom of heaven, but only the one who does the will of my Father in heaven. On that day many will say to me, 'Lord, Lord, did we not prophesy in your name, and cast out demons in your name, and do miracles in your name?' Then I will declare to them, 'I never knew you; go away from me, you evildoers'" (Mt 7:21-23).

Here Jesus mentions three extraordinary charisms. Even if we exercise extraordinary gifts in his name, and are effective in doing so, this does not guarantee a place in the kingdom. There must be obedience to the will of God. The implication is that those who were prophesying in his name, casting out demons in his name, and performing miracles in his name, were charlatans, misusing the gifts for their own glory, since they were not submitted in their hearts to the word of God and living by his will. Jesus goes on to tell the parable of the man who built his house on sand, and when the rain, the floods and the wind came it fell because it was not securely founded on rock. Our charismatic gifting in itself will not save us; rather it will be faith and surrender to the will of God.

The second quality of sanctity is humility. When we experience charisms we can become quite excited and elated that through the fire of God touching our lives his power is being brought to others. We can subtly begin to think that the glory is mine, that I have proprietary ownership over this gift, that in fact I am quite powerful. Humility is the antidote; standing in the truth of our nothingness, knowing that everything is gift from God. The perspective of humility protects me from drawing attention to myself, but rather making sure Jesus gets all the glory. One of the foremost figures in international healing ministry used to refer to himself as simply "the donkey carrying Jesus into Jerusalem". Another used to introduce herself as simply a "signpost pointing towards Jesus". Without humility the charisms run out of control. One image for this is to call humility the "insulator" for the electricity of the Spirit which is poured out into the Church through the manifestation of the charisms.[51] The higher the voltage of current running through a conductor the greater the insulation must be. So it is that the more intense the rush of the Spirit through God's instruments using the charisms, the greater the humility required. When there is humility the current of divine electricity can pass freely through the person without losing its power.

Humility is important since we can become envious of others' charisms and hungrily desire charisms that the Lord has not given to us. We need to remember that a charism is a particular way the Spirit has been given to us for a good purpose. No one receives all the charisms. We must humbly live within the body, sharing our own charism and gladly receiving from the charisms of others. None of us has everything, but only a little piece of the whole. Alone we cannot get it all together; but together we have it all. There is no place for self-sufficiency.

The third and most important quality of holiness is practical love. St Paul instructs us on this. After listing the gifts of the Spirit, he encourages us to "strive for the higher gifts", but he intends to show us "a way that is better than any of them" (1 Cor 12: 31). This is the way of love. If I exercise a charism even in a spectacular way, but am without love, the charism "will do me no good whatever". If I love the Church, and use my charism for the Church, then I am not holding on to my charism for myself, rather it is *for others*. I don't own my charism, but it is for the Church. In another sense, I own *all* the charisms, even if I only exercise some, because they belong to the

Church not to me. The charism of one is the charism of all. Thérèse of Lisieux had a marvellous insight when reflecting on this text (1 Cor 12:31-13:7). She realized that none of the charisms, no matter how wonderful they are, can be exercised authentically without love. There are different parts to the body of Christ, and so different charisms. But the body has a heart, and it is the function of the heart to love. She saw her vocation to be quietly in the loving heart of the Church, and so being one with all the ministries, and in a sense owning all the ministries.[52]

8

COMFORTS THE AFFLICTED

The Lord is close to the broken-hearted; the crushed in spirit he saves (Ps 34:19).

One of the main titles for the Holy Spirit is the *"Paraclete"*. The famous hymn, the *Veni Creator Spiritus*, invokes the Holy Spirit as "You who are named *Paraclete*, gift of God most high." What does this mean? In the tradition the word has been interpreted in two ways, as Advocate and as Comforter. An advocate is one who intercedes and defends. Ultimately the work of the Spirit as Advocate is also our comfort. As Advocate the Holy Spirit stands by us in times of persecution and trouble, defending us, and witnessing through us to the truth of Jesus. He also defends us against the Evil one, who is "the accuser of the brethren", bringing condemnation upon us from without, and stirring up self-accusing thoughts within our hearts. The Holy Spirit comes to defend us against all accusation which would tear us down and diminish us in our own eyes or in the eyes of others. In this way by being our Advocate he is also our Comforter. While the Evil one does all he can to have us demeaned and discouraged, the Holy Spirit is constantly working to build us up and to bring the encouragement we need. The voice of the Evil one lacerates us with negative thinking and self-condemning ideas, belittling us and feeding us with lies about ourselves, about others and about God. The Holy Spirit, on the other hand, feeds us with the truth that sets us free, reminding us of our personal worth and dignity established in Christ.

By the Holy Spirit's action we can shut out from our minds the lies of the "old self" stirred up by the "father of lies", and as a new creation we can listen to the words of life spoken in our hearts by the Father of life.

The Consolation of God

The Holy Spirit brings us the consolation of God most high. The prophet Isaiah encouraging the people of Israel, who were suffering in exile, speaks the word of the Lord to be received in the Spirit, "Comfort, O comfort my people, says your God. Speak tenderly to Jerusalem and cry to her that she has served her term, that her penalty is paid" (Is 40:1). The promise of God for the exiles is for a future full of hope, "So the ransomed of the Lord shall return, and come to Zion with singing; everlasting joy shall be upon their heads; they shall obtain joy and gladness, and sorrow and sighing shall flee away. *I am he who comforts you*, why then are you afraid?" (Is 52:11-12). Here is the Lord God defining himself. This is what he will be known for; the consolation of his people. He will comfort us with maternal affection, "As a mother comforts her child, so I will comfort you; you shall be comforted in Jerusalem" (Is 66:13).

In the early Church, after the Resurrection of Jesus, the Holy Spirit was experienced as the Comforter. The early Christians experienced the Holy Spirit as their friend and ally, their defender and their solace in time of trouble and persecution, and their consolation in their daily life. We are told in the Acts of the Apostles that after a time of initial persecution the Church throughout Judea, Galilee and Samaria had peace and was built up. "Living in the fear of the Lord and in the comfort (*paraclesis*) of the Holy Spirit, it increased in numbers" (Acts 9:31). John the evangelist, who is writing out of his own experience of having known the Holy Spirit, recalls the words of Jesus at the Last

Supper, "I will ask the Father and he will give you another *Paraclete* (Comforter) to be with you forever. This is the Spirit of truth, whom the world cannot receive, because it neither sees him nor knows him. *You know him, because he abides with you, and he will be in you*" (Jn 14:15-17). The early Church was keenly aware of and grateful for the infilling presence of the Holy Spirit, who was their strength in weakness, their comfort in afflictions, their light in the darkness, their witness of God's love in times of trial, their joy in times of sorrow, and their peace in times of anxiety. They experienced the Spirit as a lively presence in their lives, someone with whom they were "at home". This helped them not to feel abandoned when troubles came, but to stand firm in times of adversity. They knew they were not alone. Jesus had promised at the Last Supper,

> I will not leave you orphaned; I am coming to you. In a little while the world will no longer see me, but you will see me; because I live, you also will live. On that day you will know that I am in my Father, and you in me, and I in you (Jn 14:18-20).

In this text Jesus was comforting his apostles. He knew they were sorrowful and troubled about his departure from them. He was preparing them for the difficulties ahead. He kept reassuring them that they will not be left desolate, but the Advocate, the Helper, the Comforter, will be within them, providing all the help they need, protecting them and providing them with knowledge of the truth. He encourages them, "It is to your advantage that I go away, for if I do not go away, the *Paraclete* will not come to you; but if I go, I will send him to you" (Jn 16:7). The Comforter will provide the love and the power of the risen Christ which will sustain them through all their hardships and suffering.

Comfort one another

The Holy Spirit does not only act as Comforter in our own soul, but he prompts us and empowers us to comfort one another in times of tribulation. Paul wrote, "Blessed be the God and Father of our Lord Jesus Christ, the Father of mercies and the God of all consolation, who consoles us in all our affliction, so that we may be able to console those who are in any affliction with the consolation with which we ourselves are consoled by God" (2 Cor 1:3-4). In this passage the Greek word from which *Paraclete* is derived is used five times. Consolation to those in sorrow and lamentation comes from the "God of all consolation". But we who know him through his Spirit, the Comforter, are meant to bring his comfort to others; we are to be his lips, his eyes, his hands, his words. In this ministry of consolation we don't only bring our own words of encouragement, but we bring the word of God, which offers hope to the hopeless. As Francis of Assisi prayed, we want "not so much to be consoled, as to console; to be understood, as to understand; to be loved, as to love". We are truly moving in the Spirit when we are a source of encouragement to one another, always building one another up, consoling one another in times of sickness and trial. We draw alongside one another and pray with faith, sharing the word of God, and bringing hope. Through our feeble efforts God comforts and consoles the afflicted.

Prayer for Healing

One of the ways we minister the comfort of God is through prayer for healing. In these times of the new Pentecost we are recapturing the Lord's vision for his Church as the place and means where his healing work is made manifest. When people are physically sick they will naturally go to the doctor. But our ministry of consolation in the Spirit will also call us to pray in faith for physical healing. This is endorsed strongly by the Church's authority: "The sick person's desire for healing is both good and deeply human, especially when it takes the form of a trusting prayer addressed to God."[53] Again and again in the gospels we find people pressing in to Jesus for healing. He never stops them, but welcomes their requests. We are told that "everyone in the crowd was trying to touch him because power came out of him that cured them all" (Lk 6:19). The Lord's only complaint was that sometimes people who approached him for healing lacked faith. For example the father of the epileptic boy, who begged Jesus, "If you can do anything, have pity on us and help us," and Jesus replied, "If you can! Everything is possible to the one who has faith" (Mk 9:23). In these days after the resurrection the Holy Spirit continues the work of Jesus. Bodily healings are signs of the coming resurrection of the body. They are signs that God has power to heal the whole body-person, not just the soul. They witness that the body is important in the salvific plan of God.

One-third of the gospel stories are about Jesus healing and restoring the dead to life. When he sent out his apostles, he commissioned them "to proclaim the Kingdom of God and to heal" (Lk 9:2). We are told that after he ascended to the Father, the apostles, empowered by the Spirit, "preached everywhere, the Lord working with them and confirming the word by the signs that accompanied it" (Mk 16:19). These "signs and wonders", primarily physical healings, were the external witness of the Spirit to the truth of the gospel proclaimed. Healings function to draw the unbeliever to faith.

A Miracle Baby

A young couple received distressing news early in their second pregnancy. There was a problem with the child in the womb. The condition is rare, a diaphragmatic hernia. As a result the bowel was protruding through the hole in the diaphragm and getting in the way of the lungs. After much ultra-sound testing the head of foetal medicine in the hospital decided nothing could be done until the baby was born. The baby would have only 30% chance of survival after birth. The last test confirming this condition was made just ten days before the child was due to be induced. In that last week the couple organized for Mass to be celebrated at their home. It was a beautiful celebration, with great pathos, but with deep faith and willingness to trust the Lord that this little baby would survive. That is what they fervently prayed for, not realizing that the Lord would answer their prayer beyond their wildest dreams.

On the day for the induced birth there were ten medical staff, doctors and nurses from different departments, poised for action. The parents had been told that the baby would be born blue, the chest would have caved in, and the child would not be able to breathe. The doctors would have limited time to give the child a muscle relaxing drug and get the child to a breathing apparatus to assess the extent of the damage, and what prospects the child would have of survival.

To their great surprise the little boy arrived with normal colour, and he let out a wailing cry that astonished all. The doctors swung into action, dutifully performing their procedures. But after some time they realized it was not necessary. They had on their hands a perfectly healthy boy. They could not find any evidence of any physical problem at all! Praise the Lord for a miracle!

The most beautiful part of the story was the Baptism, which was celebrated before one thousand young people at the Easter Vigil Mass at the Light to the Nations pilgrimage. When the father of the little boy shared his testimony of the miraculous healing of his son you could have heard a pin drop, but when he finished speaking the young people burst into thunderous applause, which was a full recognition of the power of God at work. We saw firsthand how the Spirit brings physical healing to witness the truth to those struggling with faith. That night numerous young people responded publicly to a call to give their lives over to Jesus as their Lord and Saviour.

The Place of Suffering

But what about those with whom we pray for healing and yet are not healed? Does that mean we or they are lacking in faith? No. While the Holy Spirit is manifest in healing of the sick, he is also manifest in helping those who are sick to bear with their suffering. If they accept their suffering and offer it to the Lord for the sake of his Church, they are "completing what is lacking in Christ's afflictions for the sake of his body, that is, the Church" (Col 1:24). Suffering has been redeemed. It is no longer a sign of sharing in the guilt of Adam's sin. It is now a means of redemption for ourselves and for others. The Holy Spirit comes in our time of suffering to comfort us and to help us bear our suffering joyfully and in a hope-filled way. We become a witness to others of the patience and goodness of God. God did not overcome evil by simply annihilating it. Rather he entered it, taking it on himself, and thus rendering it no longer able to destroy us. "He took our infirmities and bore our diseases" (Mt 8:17). If the Lord does not heal us of our sicknesses it is not because we have lacked faith or because he is punishing us. Rather he is offering an even more precious gift than healing. If we are healed we will eventually become sick again, but if we undergo suffering patiently in Christ we are storing up goodness that will last for eternity.

Inner Healing

The healing work of the Spirit also brings comfort to those who need emotional or psychological healing. Our society which has lost God is consequently becoming increasingly broken with so many people suffering deep interior wounds. People suffer from profound levels of anxiety, a sense of hopelessness and despair, and lack of inner peace. They also often experience fractured relationships, and the emotional and spiritual pain of these break-downs. They need to find the healing that comes from the Good News of Jesus, who, has gone into the deepest caverns of human darkness and has now risen and brought peace. The Holy Spirit brings forgiveness, peace, and renewal to people who are suffering from damaged minds, wills and emotions. During prayer for inner healing people are led to cooperate with the Lord to let him cure and remove from their psychological make-up the things that are blocking the flow of the Spirit of love. Inner healing especially involves getting in touch with hurtful memories due to traumas from the past; then repenting of any sin involved, and bringing forgiveness to those who have sinned against us; then inviting Jesus to touch into the area of hurt, filling us with his love, and draining out of us the poison of any lingering resentment or bitterness. When we are hurting, we may need all sorts of professional counselling, but nothing can take the place of the consolation of the Holy Spirit.

The Hole in the Heart Filled

At twenty-one years of age, Robert had already been wounded by life. Growing up he had experienced his father as tough, punitive, and vindictive. Robert carried a deep wound of rejection, with loads of resentment and lack of forgiveness towards his dad. His outer *persona* hid the truth of the pain and loneliness within, and the deep search for identity and a sense of belonging. His life careered out of control as he sought to assuage the pain of loneliness by drunkenness, séances, stripping cars, and the riotous behaviour of the rugby league sub-culture. Feeling unloved and unwanted, and no girl friend around, his anger and negativity towards his father erupted all the more. One day in a burst of rage he picked up his Winchester 22 and in his mind's eye was going down the hallway, through the kitchen, to where Dad was, to shoot him. At that moment Robert lifted his eyes and they fixed upon an image of the Sacred Heart on the wall, which he had hardly noticed before. The face of Jesus was looking at him. The darkness lifted. He unloaded the gun and put it away. He was beginning to seek the Lord.

Around this time in a moment of despair he seriously contemplated suicide. As he was debriefing with the guy who rescued him from his suicidal intentions, he remembers saying, "You know the hole in my heart is so deep, that even if you poured all the oceans of the world into it, that would not be enough to fill it up."

Not long after this Robert found himself at a prayer meeting, where the preacher was speaking on experience of the love of Christ, who died for us on the Cross. At the end of the message the speaker made a call for anyone who wanted prayer to come forward. Robert knew he had to step out. The preacher asked him, "What do you want?" He answered, "I don't know. What you said spoke to me. How do I get it?" The man replied, "Open your heart!" Robert asked, "How do I do that?" The answer was, "Ask Jesus to come into your life. Close your eyes and trust." Robert opened his life to the Lord. Hands were stretched out over his head. During the prayer the Holy Spirit came in a mighty flood of love. It was overwhelming. David felt the impossible happen. The hole in his heart was being filled up, by the ocean of God's love. He had been trying to fill it with grog, deep sea fishing in his eighteen-foot boat, mountaineering, money, the purchase of property – but these things didn't fill the hole. Now it was filling with the love of God poured into his soul by the Holy Spirit.

Then the Lord went deeper into the basement. A week later Robert felt a heavy oppression. He knew there was more cleansing to be done. A couple ministered to him further healing. He had a powerful deliverance from bondage to darkness due to being involved in séances, ouija boards, and other occult practices. One manifestation of the oppression had been demonic dreams. Now after the deliverance ministry they disappeared.

After his baptism in the Spirit Robert also submitted himself for inner healing in relation to his father. He was drawn to repent of the way he had dishonoured and disrespected his father. Before his father died he was able to tell his dad that he loved him. To his surprise his father then shared with Robert that he had been praying for him. Robert's healing also came from forgiving others in his life who had offended him and asking their forgiveness for his offence against them. The Spirit brought genuine reconciliation.

The Assurance of the Spirit

All healing prayer, whether for physical, emotional or spiritual healing, is about believing in God's love and communicating his love to others. When we experience God's love we find healing in the depth of our being, and at all levels of our being. This is why the Holy Spirit, who is the love of God poured into our hearts, is the healer, bringing consolation to all who call upon him. God's love for us cannot increase, since it is total, perfect, and completely unconditional. Nor can it decrease, since it is constant and everlasting. In the embrace of God's love we come to realize we are totally acceptable to him, and that he has a unique plan and purpose for our life. The Holy Spirit wants to bring this assurance to our hearts.

Paul speaks of the Spirit as the *arrabon*, that is, the "guarantee" or "pledge" or "down payment" or "first instalment" of the redemption won for us in Jesus, and of the inheritance kept for us in heaven. The

Spirit has claimed us as his own. We belong to God. Paul says that it is God who has established us in Christ and has anointed us, "by putting his seal on us and giving us his Spirit in our hearts as a first instalment" (2 Cor 1:22). In ancient times, when a down payment was made on a purchase you did not have an opportunity to default on further payments. It was a water-tight guarantee. That is how the Spirit has claimed us for God. As far as God is concerned, there is absolutely no defaulting on this purchase. Elsewhere Paul says the Holy Spirit is "the pledge (*arrabon*) of our inheritance toward redemption as God's own people" (Eph 1:14). We have a guarantee of an inheritance that is imperishable, kept in heaven for us (see 1 Pet 1:3-4). The Holy Spirit's comfort is not an occasional reality. It is not a "fair weather" friendship. He is completely dedicated to us, dwelling within us to give us assurance in times of doubt, confusion, and possible disillusionment. His indwelling presence is the ground of our hope, which is not based on wishful thinking or sentimental longing, but on the fact that we belong to God, in Christ, through the power of the Holy Spirit. This sure guarantee of our salvation is the anchor in any storm, "the assurance of things hoped for and the conviction of things not seen" (Heb 11:1).

Free from Anxiety

Anxiety is the sickness of this age. Some would maintain the deepest fear that assails us is the fear of death. "We are afraid of anything that diminishes who we are. Any slight foretaste of death, any intimation of our fragile nature, any reminder of the short and narrow confines of our existence – all these things frighten us. Rather than face them, we sell out to values that corrupt our lives. Thus, we are in bondage."[54] We are told in Hebrews that Christ came to be one like us in all things, sharing in our destiny to die, "so that he might destroy the one who has the power of death, that is, the devil, and free those who all their lives were held in slavery by the fear of death" (Heb 2:14). Without the victory of Christ we are doomed to experience death as loss and disaster, and all our lives we will be bound by an anxiety, which may never be understood, but is rooted in a fear of death.

The advertising companies play on this weakness in us. The message is subtle. Drinking a certain beer promises power in your life, happiness and sexual conquest. Advertisements promise to delay the inevitability of diminishment and death. There used to be a popular bumper sticker, "The one who dies with the most toys wins." Life is meaningless, get as much pleasure and fill your life with material things. Even though you win because you have the most toys, you still die. Maybe in today's youth culture a new bumper sticker could be "The one who dies having had the most experiences wins." Chalking up the wildest extreme sport experience or the most outrageously dangerous mountain trek, or travelling the world to grasp the ultimate kick, whatever it may be, it is all a race against death. Somewhere underneath all of this is a deep anxiety. There is no peace. Anger, greed, brittle relationships, immorality, confusion especially in the area of sexuality, can be symptomatic of this loss of peace. When humanity rebels against God, and is not submitted to his ways, we find ourselves living anxious lives with little meaning and purpose.

Wherever the devil has a hold there is disturbance, disquiet, unrest, and anxiety. Wherever the Holy Spirit is present there is peace. When Jesus rose from the dead he had already been to the darkest hole of human lostness and alienation. Now having won the victory over death, as the Risen Lord, he stands amidst his disciples. The first words he spoke were, "Peace be with you." He showed them the wounds in his hands and feet to assure them of his sacrifice. Then he breathed on them the Holy Spirit, the Breath of God. He had promised them at the Last Supper that he would send the Holy Spirit, and bring peace, "Peace I leave you; my peace I give you. I do not give to you as the world gives. Do not let your hearts be troubled, and do not let them be afraid" (Jn 14:27). Now that he has conquered death, he breathes the Spirit of peace upon them.

The Holy Spirit frees us from all fear. If anxiety is the peril of our age, the Holy Spirit is the hope of our age. Paul assures us, "For you did not receive a spirit of slavery to fall back into fear, but you have received a Spirit of adoption" (Rom 8:15). By this Paul means that we have been adopted by the Father, and made sons and daughters, empowered to call him "Abba!" That is, the Spirit within us convinces us that we can utterly trust God, that we can put our lives in his hands and not be afraid. We know in the depth of our being that God is our Father, and he is on our side. We will no longer be inclined to listen to the whispering lies of the tempter who will try to convince us that God is not trustworthy, that our joy will be found elsewhere.

The Fruit of Peace

This inner peace is found when, through the indwelling of the Spirit, our hearts rest in Christ. Jesus said, "Come to me all you who labour and are heavy burdened, and I will give you rest" (Mt 11:28). The soul is meant to rest in the Lord at all times, even when it experiences the turmoil of temptations, the threats of persecution, or the calamities of life. This inner tranquility is like living in the eye of a storm. There may be much tumult and disturbance on the surface but in the depth of the heart one remains at peace. This is the work of the Spirit. However, like any fruit of the Spirit, as with the virtues, we must bring our wills to cooperate with the Holy Spirit so this inner peace becomes an habitual quality of the heart that we never lose. We may still experience struggle, temptations, disorderly desires and rebellious feelings at times, but we will pass through these without too much bother, since the heart has found its true resting place.

What is this resting place of the human heart? Where is the heart most safe and secure? The answer is simple – in the will of God. Underneath all anxiety there is a rebellious spirit, a self-sufficient spirit, seeking to make its own way according to its own designs. There is a line in Dante's *Divine Comedy* which sums it up: "In His will is our peace."[55] We find the same admonition in Augustine's *Confessions*, "In your good will is our peace."[56] The secret of our peace is found in our point of rest. We must find our rest in God. When we ask the Holy Spirit to give us peace we are asking the Spirit to help us at all times to do the will of the Father, just as Jesus did. So the answer is in trust and obedience. We seek to trust in "Abba", Father, no matter what happens in our lives, no matter what testing may come our way. As we read in Isaiah: "You keep him in perfect peace, O Lord, whose mind is stayed on you, because he trusts in you. Trust in the Lord always, for the Lord God is an everlasting rock" (Is 26:3). We are to live our lives with our mind fixed on the Lord, and seeking to do his will. Peace is found in a child-like trust in God. "Truly I have set my soul in silence and peace. A weaned child on its mother's breast, even so is my soul" (Ps 131:2). We must constantly be positioning ourselves as a child in the arms of our loving God.

We must cling to the will of God in humble obedience, no matter what. We follow the example of Jesus, "Learn from me, for I am gentle and humble of heart, and you will find rest for your souls" (Mt 11:29). This is no easy matter, since there is a core of rebellion in each of us. We would like to shape our lives independently of the will of God. But tranquillity comes to the soul when we are in God's will, when we have surrendered our lives to him. But this is a daily task, since our freedom is involved. Paul says, "where the Spirit of the

Lord is there is freedom" (2 Cor 3:17). Human freedom is not found outside of the will of God, but rather in obedience to God's will. The Spirit of God dwelling within us coaches us to conform our will to God's will. At times we may experience a battle with Satan in the wilderness, and a tortuous struggle in our own personal Gethsemane, but the obedience of Jesus is our redemption. The Holy Spirit will enflame us with such a love for God that we only want to do what pleases him. In his will is our peace.

9

DELIVERANCE FROM EVIL

Blessed be the Lord, my rock, who trains my arms for battle, who prepares my hands for war (Ps 144:2).

When we become more aware of the activity of the Holy Spirit in our lives, we also become more alert to the activity of Satan and evil spirits. We are more acutely in touch with the reality of the spiritual battle. The light of the Holy Spirit unmasks the influence of evil forces. Exhorting us to "be strong in the Lord and in the strength of this power" Paul urges us to "put on the whole armor of God, so that you may be able to stand against the works of the devil". This is a call to vigilance. The battle with the powers of darkness is real. We cannot opt out of this or pretend it is not happening. "For our struggle is not against enemies of flesh and blood, but against ... spiritual forces of evil in the heavenly places" (Eph 6:10-12). The Holy Spirit wakes us out of our stupor, and keeps us armed against the work of Satan and evil spirits.

The Reality of Evil

In today's highly secularized culture in which everything is measured by empirical science, people readily dismiss the existence of the devil and evil spirits as antiquated mythology, or mediaeval obscurantism. Satan is passed off as a symbol of the collective unconscious, or of our collective alienation. Satan and evil spirits are just a fanciful personification of the unknown causes of all our troubles. After all we now have the benefit of psychological analysis, which will explain for us all we need to know about our interior afflictions.

But in the light of the Holy Spirit we are led to affirm strongly the Church's teaching on Satan and evil spirits. Angels are God's creation, made to adore God and be his messengers. Satan and evil spirits were originally created by God as good angels, but they rebelled against him. Now they have irrevocably fallen, and totally hate God. They cannot directly oppose God, so they attack his creatures. When we hear of consummate evil in despotic regimes such as those of Hitler, Stalin, Pol Pot, Idi Amin, and so many others, it suggests to us the existence of a malevolent agent behind such atrocities. But possibly the most cogent evidence for the existence of Satan is not in those circumstances of hatred, violence, lust, murder, and horrible darkness where this despicable agent is most "at home". Rather the clearest evidence for the existence of "personalized" evil is in the lives of the saints, where the Evil one has no home at all.

With the saints there can be no ambiguity. When Satan comes against them it is black against white. He cannot be camouflaged. In contrast, the worst human atrocities could possibly be explained by other influences on the perpetrators. In these circumstances there is a certain obscurity to Satan's presence; he can hide and have the blame cast on the perpetrators alone. In the lives of the saints it is different. There the devil has to come out into the open, to stand out "against the light". The darkness of the devil's activity strongly contrasts with the light shining in the holy lives of recognized saints such as John Vianney or Padre Pio. These saints were often tormented by the devil and evil spirits. The radiance of their sanctity made the devil come out of his hiding place, but this agent of malice was rendered impotent in his attempts to prevent the work of God. All of the saints testify to the struggle they had against this "personal" power that has a perverse intelligence and will. They were victorious in Christ. They were full of the Holy Spirit who gives us complete assurance of victory over the Evil one. They were one with Jesus, the Holy One of God, who was confronted with the temptations of Satan in the desert, and prevailed.

The Victory in Christ

The light of the Holy Spirit gives clarity and a firm assurance that Christ has won the victory. Satan is a defeated foe. The powers of darkness cannot prevail over us if we stand in Christ, and rely upon the power of the Holy Spirit. The gospels attest to Jesus routing the "strong man's" house and definitively conquering the kingdom of Satan (Mt 12:29). Up to this time the "strong man" was in control, and the kingdom of darkness ruled. But now the Stronger One has come to break the power of Satan, to usher in the Kingdom of light and love, to lift the heavy oppression of the power of evil upon mankind as a result of the fall. Christ had resisted the temptations thrown against him in the wilderness (Mt 4:1-8). He exercised authority over demons, "If it is by the Spirit of God that I cast out demons, then the Kingdom of God has come to you" (Mt 12:27-29). By the power of the Holy Spirit Jesus set free those captive to evil spirits. St Basil put it simply, "In the presence of the Holy Spirit the devil lost his power."[57]

Then by dying on the Cross Jesus definitively overcame the power of Satan and evil spirits. On the Cross he cancelled the debt that we had to pay. "He set this aside, nailing it to the cross. He disarmed the rulers and authorities and made a public example of them, triumphing over them in it" (Col 2:15). And then God the Father raised him from the dead, and seated him at his right hand, "far above all rule and authority and power and dominion ... he has put all things under his feet" (Eph 1:21-22). So while insisting on the existence of Satan and evil spirits, and knowing that the devil was "a murderer from the beginning", intent upon our destruction, we are in no way fazed by this reality. The power of the Spirit of God is within us, and through his Spirit, we know that victory is ours, as long as we remain vigilant and keep on the armor of God.

Temptation

The most prevalent way the evil spirits act in our lives is by temptation.[58] As from the beginning the Evil one is the seducer, the "father of lies" and the "prince of darkness". As in the garden of Eden, he deals in deception and confusion, causing a dark cloud to come over the mind. His offerings are always attractive, sometimes quite glamorous and alluring. It is important in the hour of temptation to remain calm. Anxiety is a great killer in the spiritual life. We simply cling to Jesus, call on the power of the Holy Spirit, and rebuke the temptation in the name of Jesus. We need to remember that the Evil one is like a false lover who will seek to do his seductive work in secret. He likes to work in darkness. If he is exposed he will flee. Thus, it is good to keep everything in the light with one's spiritual director. Also remember that, even though he is a formidable opponent, he is actually a coward. If we stand up to him, clothed in the armor of Christ, he will flee. "Like a roaring lion your adversary the devil prowls around, looking for someone to devour. Resist him, steadfast in your faith" (1 Pet 5:8-9). And it is important not to forget that the Evil one is like a shrewd military commander who will attack at the weakest spot of your defences. We must always be vigilant, and guard where we are most vulnerable.[59]

We need to use prayer, fasting and the sacramental life as a protection against temptation. It is also advisable to regularly do an examination of conscience and make use of the sacrament of

Reconciliation. This sacrament provides the forgiveness of sins, but also the strength we need to resist temptations in the future. We should invoke often the mercy of God, especially calling the blood of Jesus to wash clean the areas of our lives where we most struggle. The tradition of the Jesus Prayer can help, since we are invoking the name of Jesus which has power to protect from demons and bring healing to our lives. "Lord Jesus Christ, Son of the Living God, have mercy on me a sinner." Most of all we need the Eucharist. As Pope John Paul II taught, "Every Eucharistic celebration is stronger than all the evil in the universe; it means real, concrete accomplishment of the Redemption."[60] In Eucharist, more than anywhere else, do we find the victory of Christ, and in its whole-hearted celebration we can most fruitfully avail ourselves of its power.

Oppression

Another way we struggle with evil is called *oppression*. This is when evil has a hold on an area of our life, and we cannot control it. Maybe it is an addiction, binge drinking, stealing, habitual sexual disorder, pornography or some other captivity. We experience the power of an overwhelming attraction to do something that is damaging to us. Giving in to the craving provides a moment of satisfaction, but then the onset of guilt and shame drives us back again to the sedative. These obsessions are destructive and may well have a spiritual dimension as well as physical and psychological dimensions. As well as counselling, there is usually need for inner healing prayer, in the context of which a person can be delivered from the hold of an evil spirit. When there are besetting sinful patterns in our life, especially of a more perverse kind, a stronghold of an evil spirit may need to broken.

There are many ways we can expose ourselves to the powers of darkness, and hence come under oppressive harassment. When a person is involved in sexual perversions, pornography or the use of drugs they have left their soul open to being oppressed by an evil spirit. A wilful rejection of the Church can also leave a person vulnerable to evil influence, since the person has sinned through unbelief, and no longer enjoys the protection of the Church. Dabbling in the occult, which is quite popular in today's culture, is a definite opportunity for demonic activity. Any form of divination – séances, fortune telling, Ouija board, Tarot Cards – is a sin against faith and invites evil spirits. Even white magic – Wicca – a supposed source of healing, can open someone to the influence of demons. People who engage in esoteric spiritual practices through the New Age movement can also provide access for the activity of evil spirits.

Often people suffer from oppression as a result of deep hurts of the past that can leave a person with various kinds of obsessive fears, memories of rejection or deep injustices done them by family members or other significant persons, or a sense of self-hate and feeling worthless. Some suffer enduring bitterness and resentment, irrational jealousy, and other torments of the soul. These deep wounds or traumas of the past can provide a point of entry for an evil spirit to exert influence. Experience shows that the deliverance ministry is best exercised in the context of prayer for inner healing. Unless the wounds of the past are healed through the loving touch of Jesus deep within the person, any attempt to deliver from the influence of evil spirits will be short-lived, since the unhealed area remains vulnerable to further manipulation by the powers of darkness. All healing is meant to be integral to the whole person, that is at all levels of the person, physical, emotional and spiritual.

Trapped no More; Free at Last[61]

By the age of 15, David Payne was experimenting with drugs. He had been introduced to them by older guys. "I was doing a lot of speed, loads of acid, smoking a lot of dope." Much to the dismay of his parents, he was drawn into the Punk rock scene, "My hair got shorter, the music got louder, and the drugs got harder." Then romance arrived. For the sake of his girl, he dropped the drugs. He started to be successful in business and began to live the high life. But he had built his life around this woman. The relationship was "the driving force of my life". Then after six years she walked out on him for another guy. David's life was shattered. They had not been married, but she had been everything for him. He felt "utterly betrayed and crushed". He attempted suicide by overdosing on sleeping pills, but thankfully did a botched job of it. "I couldn't think of one motivation to take the next breath. I'd tried money. I'd tried romance. I'd been betrayed. I'd tried everything. Nothing had worked."

The intense inner pain, the emotional and mental torment was too much. He turned again to chemicals to numb the pain. "And so with a vengeance and a death wish I turned back, this time to hard stuff called methadone, a heroin substitute, a very clever drug! It makes you feel alive, like a hero, which is where the word heroin comes from … it numbed the pain real good and made life bearable." But after a few months he was addicted. "We were playing gigs in warehouses at night, drug dealing, driving cars out of our brains, dodging the police. I was sleeping around with women and I didn't even know their names. I caught diseases and there was just darkness in my life."

David's mother kept feeding him Christian books. Every time he came home for money or food he would come away with yet another book or tape. But he never read them. But one day when he was bored he picked up one of the books. It was called, *Run Baby Run*, by Nicky Cruz – a true story of a skinny preacher, name David Wilkerson, who in New York had convinced hardened gang leaders, addicted to drugs, like Nicky that "Jesus can set you free". David felt a tingle of hope rise within him. Then he read another one of Mum's books called *Chasing the Dragon*, which means smoking heroin, which he was doing by that time. This true story is of a Scottish woman who ventured among the drug triads in Hong Kong, and offered them the baptism in the Spirit. They were able to be released from drugs by the power of the Holy Spirit, with no "cold turkey", no "withdrawal symptoms"! Again David felt hope rising. But could it really happen to him, in East Finchley, London?

It began to dawn on David that he was killing himself, and death would not be a release, but entry into hell. "The hell that I was living was going to continue after death and get worse." He was terrified. He went home to his mother. "I was desperate and I was ready to try anything, even the most uncool thing I could think of, which was to try God. I'd tried everything else – sex, drugs, rock & roll, crime." He asked his mother, "Where is this God?" Relieved, she informed him about a talk coming up by a Hells Angel who had been converted to Christianity. The testimony of the Hells Angel spoke powerfully to him. It was as if this man had lived through the hell of his own journey. And he was claiming Jesus had set him free. At the end of the talk the speaker called for three people in the hall who had to meet the Lord that night. He called them to stand up right then and there. David knew it was him, but gripped his chair, "No way!" But then the Holy Spirit moved on him. He was standing. Later he recalled it was "the most courageous thing I have ever done". The speaker led him through a prayer asking for forgiveness for his sins, and then faith in Jesus as the Son of God. David said, "It was as if something was lifted from me there and then. I stood there and hope burst into my life. I felt a weight lift off my shoulders, the heaviness of guilt and despair." But this was just a beginning. He was still addicted to drugs and to the lifestyle that went with it. He says, "I had experienced love and forgiveness that night, but I had yet to experience power." He went back to his mother. She told him, "You need to go to a prayer meeting; there is one happening next week. There you will find the power."

So next week David and his friends headed on a wet night in February to the prayer meeting. "The door opened and to our horror, instead of being greeted by pretty girls with guitars, as we had expected, there were about forty middle-aged Irish ladies and three nuns. Before we could turn and run down to the pub, which was our instant reaction, they kind of grabbed us, hugged us and took us in." Feeling trapped in the place, with the nuns blocking the doorway, they began to make fun of the old folk songs the ladies were singing. David was beginning to think the whole thing was a horrible mistake, and he just wanted to smoke a joint and "get out of his head" quickly. But something changed. This is how he describes it:

> These old Irish ladies, who couldn't sing to save their lives began to sound like angels. It was as if they began to sing in a new language, all of them at once. It was harmonizing and beautiful, and we looked at their faces which were glowing. They seemed to just know that God was there, and suddenly the atmosphere changed in the hall; we could begin to sense God's presence, a power and a love all around us. Only weeks before I had tangibly experienced a presence of evil and here I was now, experiencing God. We stopped laughing and listened in awe. This strange language is called singing in tongues.

As they were leaving the ladies grabbed them and said, "Listen, God can change your life." They nervously laughed and left quickly.

But they came back again the next week. They were still trapped in drugs, but they implicitly knew they had encountered something that they needed.

On the third visit David finally let them pray with him to be set free from drugs. He admits that while he wanted to be free, he was very nervous; because "if God didn't show up, there was nothing left for me. I would have to return to emptiness. And, I felt unworthy; maybe God wouldn't come because of all the bad things I'd done and said. I felt terribly confused". Yet he let them pray. The ladies began to pray with him in tongues. "It was as if God just started to flow into me, as if somebody was just pouring precious warm liquid. I felt the insides warm up, and it was as if the emptiness – that hole that had been inside of me since the age of fourteen – just filled up. What is more, I began to speak in tongues too. I began to thank God, praying inside, saying 'God, give me everything. I am desperate. I want it all. I want to be powerful. I want to be free. Fill me up. Come Holy Spirit. Do your stuff!' ... I felt set free. At last!"

> We left that place buzzing, floating out. I knew I was free. Free from drug addictions, free from the other crap, the sleeping around and all that stuff that I didn't want to do any more ... I didn't need to take drugs again – no cold turkey; I had no withdrawal symptoms. I threw away my drugs and I was free. It was a miracle. I couldn't do that on my own. I would have been on the floor weeping after two days! I was trapped no more. More than that, I really met Jesus. I suddenly knew that Jesus Christ is real. I began a relationship, a deep friendship with him, began to talk to him, experience him and heard his voice in me, speaking, encouraging and gently leading me. That emptiness and loneliness that I had always experienced had gone.

Prior to this time whether he had been stoned on drugs or in bed with a beautiful woman, he still knew he was alone. "When my head hit the pillow it was just me. I had to face my life and all of the struggles alone. Suddenly that had changed. No longer was I lonely on the inside." Now many years later since his baptism in the Spirit, David is able to claim, "I have never felt empty like I did before. I have had tough times, but ultimately, deep down inside, I know God is with me and his Spirit, his power, is flowing through me."

David Payne now spends his life sharing the amazing news of God's healing love. He is the Director of CaFE (Catholic Faith Exploration) which produces DVDs for parishes and schools. These resources have been widely distributed in many English-speaking countries.

The Kingdom of Light and the Kingdom of Darkness

The story of David's deliverance speaks of the power of God through the Holy Spirit which breaks the reign Satan in our lives. Jesus made a beautiful promise to his apostles at the Last Supper about the Holy Spirit, the other *Paraclete,* "When he comes, he will prove the world wrong about sin and righteousness and judgment; ... about judgment, because *the ruler of this world has been condemned*" (Jn 16:6-11). When Jesus had died and risen the Holy Spirit would make it very clear that Satan had been defeated. He would reveal that Jesus' death and resurrection had accomplished definitively victory over the kingdom of darkness. Earlier in John's gospel Jesus had pronounced, "Now is the judgment of this world; now *the ruler of this world will be driven out.* And when I am lifted up from the earth, I will draw all people to myself" (Jn 12:31-32). The Holy Spirit would be sent to convince the disciples that the Enemy had been overcome, and to empower them to have utter confidence when they are in struggle. As St Augustine said in one of his commentaries, "And so it is the Holy Spirit who trains our hands for battle and our fingers for war."[62]

We share through Baptism in the kingly anointing of Jesus, who resisted the temptation of Satan in the desert, and cast out demons in the power of the Spirit. He ushered in the Kingdom of light which defeated the kingdom of darkness. Our greatest defence against the wiles of the Evil one is in our submission to the Lord. In the wilderness, Jesus, through submission to the Father's will, freed himself from Satan so that he could then free us from Satan. Jesus bound Satan and cast him completely out of his life, and then set about his mission of bringing the Good News to the poor, "healing all those oppressed by the devil".

By the outpouring of the Holy Spirit at Pentecost Jesus gave his Church the same power over the forces of darkness. In the Acts of the Apostles we see the early Church continuing the ministry of Jesus in the power of the Spirit, fulfilling his command to cast out demons in his name (Mk 16:17-18). For example, in Phillip's ministry in Samaria we are told "unclean spirits came shrieking out of many who were possessed" (Acts 8:7). Paul ordered an unclean spirit to come out of a slave-girl who was a fortune teller (Acts 16:16). In Ephesus some of the believers who had been using spells and practising magic collected all their books and made a bonfire of them (Acts 19:18-19).

Liberation from a Curse

From when she was a few months old, Samantha had suffered with chronic eczema, a persistent humiliating skin disease. Now at the age of twenty-one she felt the stigma of the disease acutely, and thought that people were always staring at her. She says, "The eczema began to define who I was; I was a fearful, anxious and tense person. I was self-conscious of my skin and battled with my self- image as well as my body-image. My eczema held me back from doing many things; like eating certain foods, swimming in chlorinated pools and sleeping over at my friends' houses." Samantha's parents had been searching for remedies, but the condition was worsening. She found it so difficult to believe in God since he had allowed such a thing to happen to her. Yet while at a week long Summer School, designed to help young people grow in faith and discipleship, she felt the need to seek healing from the Lord. She stepped out in faith and asked an experienced healing team to pray with her.

During the prayer for inner healing those who were praying with Samantha sensed there was a blockage to her healing. In Samantha's words, "As I was being prayed over, the Holy Spirit revealed to the prayer team that the cause of my eczema was a curse placed on my family generations down the line, of which my family and I were completely unaware. The bonds of this curse were cut as well as anything else that Spirit revealed, including the spirit of timidity." When a simple prayer was made in the name of Jesus for the curse to be broken Samantha was completely healed of her eczema. This physical healing was an outward expression of her inner healing. Now released from bondage to an evil spirit's influence she says, "I have become the person God wants me to be; I am no longer fearful, anxious or timid. I am now able to live fully and completely in His victory." Now that she feels nothing is holding her back Samantha has signed up to give a year to the Lord in an evangelizing team ministry working with young people in Catholic schools. This is her way of giving thanks to God for her liberation from bondage.

Baptism into the Victory of Christ

The early Church found it necessary to make prayers for exorcism part of the ritual of Christian initiation. The Roman ritual for infant baptism that was in use up until Vatican II had a pre-baptismal exorcism, "Go out of this child, unclean spirit, and leave place for the Holy Spirit." The rite today carries a similar sense when there is first the oil of catechumens, which is an exorcism rite, by which the child is claimed from the powers of darkness, and then the oil of chrism, which is for the anointing of the Spirit.

The *Rite of Christian Initiation of Adults*, during Lent, includes within it three ritual "scrutinies" which are intended to purify the catechumens in mind and heart, and to strengthen them against temptation, and to make them firm in their decision for Christ. "By exorcism they are freed from the effects of sin and from the influence of the devil, and they are strengthened in their spiritual journey and open their hearts to receive the gifts of the Saviour."[63] Cyril of Jerusalem of the fourth century, speaking about the initiation of adults, gives testimony, "It happened that a demon, whom many had been unable to bind, was overcome by the words of one man's prayer because of the Holy Spirit who dwelt in him. The very breath of the exorcist, though invisible, was like fire to the malign spirit."[64] In the celebration of Baptism, both for children and for adults, the ritual has a threefold renunciation of Satan and all influences of the powers of darkness, followed by a threefold confession of faith in Father, Son and Holy Spirit. Every Easter we renew this renunciation of Satan and confession of faith. We claim again the power of our Baptism into the victory of Christ and new life in the Spirit.

Put on the Armour of God

In the renewal of our Baptism we seek to walk in the light, living in the victory of Jesus, free from the wiles of the Devil. We are still in a spiritual battle, but we are not alone or left to our own resources. Paul tells us how to arm ourselves:

> Therefore take up the whole armour of God, so that you may be able to withstand on that evil day, and having done everything, to stand firm. Stand therefore, and fasten the belt

of truth around your waist, and put on the breastplate of righteousness. As shoes for your feet put on whatever will make you ready to proclaim the gospel of peace. With all of these, take the shield of faith, with which you will be able to quench all the flaming arrows of the evil one. Take the helmet of salvation, and the sword of the Spirit, which is the word of God. Pray in the Spirit at all times in every prayer and supplication. To that end keep alert and always persevere in supplication for all the saints (Eph 6:13-18).

Our armour is in our strength of faith in the power of the Cross of Jesus, the cleansing of his precious blood, and the invocation of his all powerful name. We are armed also by the power of the word of God which is a double-edged sword laying bare our own souls, but also being an offensive weapon against the attack of the enemy. Our armour also includes the "helmet of righteousness" which means primarily keeping ourselves uncontaminated from impure living, making sure we are not opening our minds and hearts to evil influences or compromised situations. We also have been shod with the eagerness to proclaim the gospel. When apostolic zeal wanes, we are more vulnerable to attack. But when we are faithful stewards of the gospel, the Enemy cannot touch us. And we are to be incessantly praying in the Spirit. We must pray constantly not only for ourselves but for all whom we have responsibility, and for all to whom we are bound in the Spirit. We should never underestimate the power of intercessory prayer to protect us and to empower those under our care.

The devil's whole aim is to draw us into his own disobedience against God. Our greatest protection is in our humble obedience to the will of God. We share in the victory of Jesus over Satan, which was not attained through violent or dramatic means. Rather it was achieved though humility and obedience unto death on a cross. It was not attained through human strength, but rather through human weakness and brokenness, that God's power may be made manifest. Sharing in his victory, means staying united with Jesus in humble submission to the will of the Father. It means knowing our weakness and vulnerability, and relying fully on the power of God to save and protect us. Then we have nothing to fear from the unrestrained powers of evil which may come against us. We have the assurance of Jesus that if, as Church, we are faithful to the proclamation of the gospel, the strongholds of Satan will not be able to stand against us (Mt 16:16). And we have the assurance from St Paul that "God is faithful, and he will not let you be tested beyond your strength, but with the testing he will always provide the way out so that you may be able to endure it" (1 Cor 10:13).

10
PRAYER IN THE SPIRIT

Rejoice always, pray without ceasing, give thanks in all circumstances; for this is the will of God in Christ Jesus for you (1 Thess 5:16-18).

The Life-giving Spirit

We have already opened up the image of the Holy Spirit as fire falling upon us at Pentecost and setting our hearts aflame with love. Another traditional image for the Spirit is water. Rather than the Spirit envisaged as coming down in power from on high, this image speaks of the Spirit breaking forth from within and welling up to bring fullness of life. The Scriptures give us the symbol of water springing up miraculously in desert places, as a fulfillment of God's promise of new life. The Lord promises, "I will make rivers well up on barren heights ... and turn dry ground into a water spring" (Is 41:18). The waters gushing in the desert spoke to the prophets of God's saving love, "You will draw water joyfully from the springs of salvation" (Is 12:2). One of the most striking of these prophecies about the water of life is found in Ezekiel's vision of a spring welling up in the Temple. The prophet saw the spring forming a stream flowing ever wider and deeper, as it becomes a river fertilizing the *Arabah*, which is one of the most barren landscapes in the world. Wherever the river flowed in the wilderness it was filled with living creatures of every kind, and vegetation grew plentifully on its banks; a symbol of the stream of God's saving grace, bringing fruits of new life, healing, and restoration (Ezek 47:1-12).

Undoubtedly Ezekiel's vision was being evoked by Jesus, when on the last day of the Feast of Tabernacles, he stood in the temple and cried out, "Let anyone who is thirsty come to me, and let the one who believes in me drink. As Scripture has said, 'From his breast shall flow fountains of living water'." John tells us, "He said this about the Spirit, which believers in him were to receive; for as yet there was no Spirit, because Jesus was not yet glorified" (Jn 7:17-39). The thirst deep within the human heart will be satiated by the living waters of the Spirit. It seems likely that the words "from his breast shall flow fountains of living water" refer to the living waters flowing from the heart of Jesus, pierced on the Cross by the soldier's lance. John gives eye witness testimony that blood and water flowed from the side of Christ opened up for us on the Cross (Jn 19:34-35); the blood symbolizing the price of our redemption and the water symbolizing the gift of the Spirit.

The Gift of Prayer

Earlier in John's gospel, when Jesus encounters the woman at the well, we find again this theme of the Spirit as life-giving water. Here our focus can turn specifically towards the Spirit welling up within us bringing the wonderful gift of prayer. We notice that Jesus initiates the conversation. He thirsts, and asks for water. His request for water from the woman was not only about his physical thirst. More so it was an expression of his heart desire, the heart of God himself, for union with each one of us. When she retorts with surprise and contention, Jesus says, "If you knew the gift of God, and who it is who is saying to you, 'Give me a drink', you would have asked him, and he would have given you living water" (Jn 4:10). If only we knew the immense gift of the Spirit that is being offered to us! Christ comes to meet each person and he thirsts for us. He wants union with us.

The woman replies, trying to make sense of how Jesus would give her water other than from Jacob's well which is so deep, and has such fresh, clear water available for anyone with a bucket to drink. Then Jesus gives the promise:

> Everyone who drinks of this water will be thirsty again, but those who drink of the water that I will give them will never be thirsty. The water that I will give will become in them a spring of water gushing up to eternal life (Jn 4:13-14).

How beautiful is this promise of Jesus! His thirst for us awakens in us a deep thirst for him. This is what is happening in the mysterious encounter with the Samaritan woman. As the conversation continues she finds a thirst deep within her, which she had tried to satisfy by disordered relationships. Now she finds the real and deepest focus of this desire. She is opened up to the spring of the Spirit within her heart, welling up to eternal life.

Within each of us is a deep desire for union with God, but it can often be covered over and blocked up by all sorts of pursuits that do not ultimately provide life for the soul. God's loving desire for us stirs up that deep thirst which can only be satiated in God, and he provides that living spring of the Spirit within us, bubbling up for fullness of life. Referring to the teaching of St Augustine, the *Catechism of the Catholic Church* puts it succinctly, "Whether we realize it or not, prayer is the encounter of God's thirst with ours. God thirsts that we may thirst for him."[65]

Praying in Tongues

When people experience being baptized in the Spirit they will usually at that time, or soon afterwards, begin to pray in tongues. Through the advent of this gift they find that the life of prayer is released in them more powerfully. They will experience a more immediate contact with God, and find themselves praising him with ease, and desiring to spend long times in adoration. It is as if a stone had been rolled away in the heart, releasing a new spring of life-giving water that had previously been blocked. The praises of God simply well up from the depth of the heart. Under this anointing people experience, maybe for the first time, the truth that prayer is a gift of the Spirit, and in fact, when we don't know how to pray it is the Spirit who prays within us. As Paul says, "The Spirit helps us in our weakness; for we do not know how to pray as we ought, but that very Spirit intercedes for us with sighs too deep for words. And God who searches the heart, knows what is the mind of the Spirit, because the Spirit intercedes for the saints according to the will of God" (Rom 8:26-27). No matter how broken we are, how helpless we may feel, how inadequate we are in prayer, the Spirit groans deeply within us, bestowing the gift of prayer, which is not of our own making, but of his creation.

Praying in tongues allows us to pray vocally beyond ordinary words and concepts which seem to restrict the expression of our praise and worship of God. The sounds that come are not any known language, but arise spontaneously. The person praying in tongues does not know what he or she is saying, but is only aware of saying it. They are not in a trance or ecstatic state. They remain in control of what is happening, and can decide when to start and when to stop, and are not automatically carried away by the gift. Fr George Montague, a prominent biblical scholar, gives his testimony of being released in the gift of tongues when he was baptized in the Spirit:

> As I knelt there, hearing the voices of those praying over me, I began to feel a bubbling inside. It was just there and I didn't know what to do with it. One of the ways in which I sought to release it was by finishing the last three chapters of a book I was writing – and I did it in less than three days. But

the bubbling was still there. On New Year's day, as I drove to the ranch to visit my family, I felt moved just to relax and let the bubbling come out however it would. It came out in a melody without words. Three days later, words came to fit the melody: "The Spirit of the Lord has touched my soul ..." Far from being spent by the song, the bubbling was still there. It seemed to go beyond what I could put in either melody or words. Could this be the gift of tongues?

I went to my room, closed my door, knelt down – and let go. I stopped a couple of times as if looking at myself in the mirror, and reflected how stupid this sounded. But then I tried to ignore that. I began to focus on the Lord, and then it was easier to let go. More and more came ... So that's tongues! Praising God by letting the Spirit do it in you, for you, and with you!

Since then my life has been so different, so rich, so full of inexplicable events. I have witnessed physical healing. I have witnessed the powerful inner healings of soul and Spirit – the healing of marriages and families, the healing of long-festering hatreds. But my greatest witness to the Lord's deep healing is myself. I have found a new strength and vitality, a greater willingness to risk for the Lord, a greater ability to cope with stress and chaos. I have been able to say "praise God" for the whole of my past.[66]

The Gift of Jubilation

The gift of praying in tongues can also be manifest in a communal expression of singing in tongues. This is a particularly sweet and beautiful way of worshiping the Lord. The harmony of the various sounds come together in a symphony inspired by the Spirit. It is nothing miraculous, but is often impressive to people who first encounter it, because it transcends any planned melodies or songs. It is a wonderful manifestation of the gift of thanksgiving, praise and joyful worship, which is both tranquil and yet majestic. St Paul says, "I will sing praise with the spirit, but I will sing praise with the mind also" (1 Cor 14:15). From the context we can ascertain that to "sing praise with the spirit" probably meant some kind of singing in tongues. Paul often refers to communal singing inspired by the Spirit: "Be filled with the Spirit as you sing psalms and hymns and spiritual songs among yourselves, singing and making melody to the Lord in your hearts" (Eph 5:19). Usually in charismatic gatherings the singing in tongues breaks out after the words of a familiar song have faded, and the worship of the Lord is prolonged by waves of praise in harmonious sounds as though an unseen conductor was directing it from beginning to end.

St Augustine, in his commentary on the Psalms, which are full of what he called the prayer of "jubilation", writes about singing in the Spirit beyond words:

> Singing well to God means, in fact, just this: singing to him in jubilation. What does singing in jubilation mean? It is to experience that words cannot communicate the song of the heart. Just so, singers in the harvest or at vintage or in some other fervent work, delighted with the abundant produce, and rejoicing in the very richness and exuberance of the soil, sing in exultation. They express their rapture at first in songs set to words; then, as if bursting with a joy so full that they cannot express it in set words, they abandon words and break into the free melody of pure jubilation.[67]

Here Augustine is speaking about a natural human jubilation, expressing the sheer joy of living. He saw it in the workers while harvesting, who were overflowing with joyful song. This helps us to understand the dynamics of the song of jubilation addressed to God:

> Jubilation is a certain kind of sound that points to the fact that the heart wants to express something that cannot be said in words. And to whom is this jubilation most fittingly addressed, if not to God who is ineffable? What is ineffable cannot be expressed in words, nor can it be passed over in silence. So what can one do but jubilate? For in jubilation the heart opens up to joy without words, and that joy widens out immeasurably beyond the utmost reaches of our words.[68]

Shouting the Praises of God

When we praise God in the Spirit, the focus is taken off ourselves and put upon the Lord. We praise God for who he is. The Holy Spirit anoints us and explodes the fixed categories in our minds about God. Praising God in the Spirit overcomes our inherent tendency to domesticate God. Like the Israelites in the Old Testament who turned to Canaanite house-gods, we can try to keep God as an idol in our minds. We want to be comfortable and feel we are in control. So we try to handle God our way, rather than submit to him. The Old Testament prophets were always denouncing false gods, calling Israel back to worship of the one true God. When we genuinely worship the Lord "in spirit and in truth", the Holy Spirit captivates our hearts, and we become seized by the great Mystery of who God is. We are caught up in the wonder of his infinite love, his mighty power and his surpassing glory. The cry "Alleluia!" which we can rattle off so readily, is in fact a whole-hearted joyful shout to the Lord for his greatness, might, splendour, magnificence and holiness. It is a "Holy WOW!" before the awesome mystery of God.

Often the jubilation prayer, inspired by the Spirit, is "a word of praise", which involves the whole assembly shouting the praises of God. We praise the Lord because we know his wonderful works. When the Holy Spirit fell on Cornelius' household, they began to speak in strange languages and "to proclaim the greatness of God" (Act 10:46). In gratitude for the wonders of his creation, we, who are the pinnacle of his creatures, with conscious mind, can articulate the praises of God on behalf of all living beings (Psalms 148, 150). Like Moses who sang his song of victory when the Egyptians were swallowed up by the Red Sea (Ex 15:1-21), we too sing our new song of praise in thanks for God's redeeming power. He has brought us out of darkness into his wonderful light. Once we were no people, now we are the people of God, "set apart to sing the praises of God" (1 Pet 2:9). We joyfully exalt in the Lord for his gift of salvation (Ps 40:1-4).

Within the experience of a new Pentecost, we find ourselves joining the tradition of the "festal shout", a joyful cry to the Lord. The Psalmists use this "festal shout" often, "All peoples, clap your hands, cry to God with shouts of joy!" (Ps 47:1). The word used here in Hebrew is "ruwah", which means "to split the ears with sound". The natural equivalent would be the roar of the crowd at the MCG when players take the field for the Grand Final. Another psalm says, "Happy the people who know the joyful shout!"(Ps 89:16). Here the Hebrew word is *teruwah* which is a battle cry. It is something like the ancient armies arrayed for battle, who make a roar to terrify the enemy before charging in to take the territory. That's the attitude of Christians who shout the victory of the Lord in their times of praise. "Jesus is Lord!" is not a timid, uncertain proclamation. It is a cry of victory; it is a battle cry which makes the Enemy flee.

In one of St Augustine's Easter liturgies, as Bishop of Hippo, a young man named Paulus was completely healed of a disease which he had from birth. As he stood healed before the congregation, Augustine tells us "everyone burst into a prayer of thankfulness to God. The whole church rang with the clamour of rejoicing. In the crowded church cries of joy rose up everywhere, 'thanks be to God!' 'Praise to God!' with everyone joining and shouting on all sides that the Lord has healed his people, and then with still louder voices shouting again."

The next day the young man's sister was also healed of a disease and again a "tumult of joy" burst forth. As Augustine describes:

> Such wonder rose from men and women together that the exclamations and the tears seemed as if they would never come to an end ... they shouted God's praises without words, but with such a noise that our ears could scarcely bear it. What was there in the hearts of all this clamoring crowd but the faith of Christ, for which St Stephen shed his blood.[69]

Praise and Contemplation

So far I have been expounding the way of vocal charismatic praise and worship of God. This gift is given by the Spirit, but it cannot sustain the soul without the gift of contemplation. As we have seen, the Holy Spirit awakens in us a thirst for union with God. The grace of the baptism in the Spirit flowers best in the experience of contemplation, which is a quiet resting in God. Some have set up a false dichotomy between charismatic praise and contemplation. These two modes of prayer are in no way opposed to one another. Rather, they complement one another, both flowing from the grace of our Baptism.

Many contemplatives down through the ages have experienced "jubilation of the heart", a silent intense joy which bursts forth in praise of God by the action of the Spirit. John Cassian speaks of the "prayer of fire", which is not vocal but is a "fiery outbreak, an indescribable exaltation, an insatiable thrust of the soul" towards God. This is a profoundly contemplative experience of praise. On the other hand he describes times when the monks burst into vocal exaltation as a result of this fire within: "Often through some inexpressible delight and keenness of spirit the fruit of a salutary conviction arises so that it actually breaks forth into shouts, owing to the greatness of the exaltation, which make themselves heard even in the cell of their neighbour."[70]

So the monks enjoyed jubilation in an interior way, but also gave vent to this by shouting the praises of God in exaltation. This contemplative "jubilation" of the early monks has been experienced by many friends of God down through the centuries. The depth of contemplative silence, and the profound infusion of love from the heart of God, may readily overflow in vocal praises. And vocal praises often stir the heart towards a deeper entry into communion with the Lord in silence.

The Gift of Contemplation and Adoration

Contemplation is being at rest with Jesus, a loving attentive gaze upon him, and also being aware of his loving attentive gaze upon me. The experience of baptism in the Spirit awakens a hunger for contemplation. Without the movement towards contemplation the charismatic grace would be left shallow and fruitless. For this grace to grow we need silence and solitude. Silence quietens the soul interiorly and becomes the mode by which we can encounter the living God. Like Elijah on the mountain top, we do not find the Lord in the tumultuous events of earthquake, fire and storm; rather in the gentle breeze we hear the still quiet voice of the Spirit speaking to us (1 Kings 19:9-13). We go into solitude to allow the Lord to lure our hearts to himself. The Spirit draws us out into the wilderness to speak to our innermost self (Hos 2:16). We become more aware that achievements and successes in life are empty if they are not attained in the Spirit. All of our striving for causes and seemingly important ideals, can be futile, since they reinforce a false self, which is not truly who I am in God. As the prophet proclaimed, "Not by might, not by power, but by my Spirit, says the Lord" (Zech 4:6).

The road towards contemplation involves a self-emptying of desires and attachments which are obstacles to union with God. The Spirit helps us to live in the truth, rather than in falsity and illusion. We discover our weakness and nothingness before God, but we also discover his immense love and kindness, and his power to deliver us from all that would hold us back from him. We find that he is passionately yearning for union with us. The gift of contemplation is simply yielding to that passionate embrace of the Lord, allowing ourselves to be caught up in this love, letting him take hold of us, letting him possess us. All of this is the work of the Holy Spirit. As the *Catholic Catechism* says: "The Holy Spirit, whose anointing permeates our whole being, is the interior Master of Christian prayer ... To be sure there are as many paths of prayer as there are persons who pray, but it is the same Spirit acting in all and with all."[71]

In contemplation our hearts are drawn to adore the Lord. We become more convinced by the Spirit of the beauty, splendour, and wonder of our God, how he is infinitely adorable in his glory and majesty. We also begin to yield to his unconditional and perfect love for us, and we surrender to his claim upon our lives; we give over to him our very selves. In adoration of God we are lovingly wrapped up in him, forgetful of ourselves, and delighting in his goodness. It is a death to everything that is not God, a total submission of the mind and will to him.

Worship in Spirit and in Truth

When Jesus was conversing with the woman at the well, he promised her the living water of the Spirit welling up within her for fullness of life. This is the Holy Spirit who moves within us bringing forth the gift of loving prayer with God. But when the subject of worship was raised by the woman, Jesus said,

> The hour will come – in fact it is here already – when true worshippers will worship in spirit and in truth: that is the kind of worshipper the Father wants. God is spirit, and those who worship must worship in spirit and truth (Jn 4:23-24).

What is valued highly by the Father is not our way of prayer, whatever technique we may use for our personal prayer, or whatever rituals we may use in our public worship. What it important is *not the way* of worship, but whether there is a *true worshipper*. If we the worshippers are truly led by the Spirit and genuinely honest before God, our worship will be in spirit and in truth. Jesus complained, "These people worship me with lip-service but their hearts are far from me" (Mk 7:6). Only when the heart is fully given over to the Lord, will the worship be true.

We worship in spirit and in truth when we can adore the Lord, like Francis of Assisi, who prayed all night, "My God and my all!" or like Thomas the apostle, who fell in adoration before the risen Christ, "My Lord and my God!" This is heartfelt adoration, which is the epitome of praise. In its most radiant form, adoration is the quiet simplicity of loving acceptance of God's love. This is the contemplative attitude. Ultimately, praise, contemplation, and adoration are different dimensions of the one movement, led by the Spirit, into deeper surrender of our hearts to God.

Witness of Luke and John

That the charismatic and the contemplative belong together as two experiences of the one Spirit in our lives can be confirmed from the biblical testimony. On the one hand, *Luke's account* of Pentecost in Acts involves a dynamic manifestation of charismatic praise with signs and wonders. There was a powerful wind from heaven, the noise of which filled the whole house. Fire came down from above and rested on each of them. They bounded out of the upper room bursting with joy and boldly proclaiming publicly the Good News. On the other hand *John's account*, as we have already seen, has the life-giving water of the Spirit gushing forth from the side of Christ on the Cross, a much gentler image associated with the breaking forth of water, bringing life to desert places. Then after the resurrection Jesus appears to his apostles, stilling their fears with his reassuring greeting of "Peace be with you." Then he *breathes* on them the Holy Spirit. This reminds us of how, at the dawn of creation, the Father fashioned the first man from clay and breathed on him the kiss of life. Now at the dawn of the new creation the Son breathes on us, elevating us to a share of his own life, which is life forever.

In some Eastern cultures to breathe on the face of the other is a sign of intimacy. Breath was, as it were, the soul of the person. So to breathe on another's face was to invite the other into "soul to soul" intimacy. The coming of the Spirit in John's account is quiet, personal, intimate. Whenever we take in the breath of Jesus we take his Spirit into ourselves, and we are drawn into his very life. Even though the apostles would have been full of guilt for their betrayal, and ashamed that they had failed Jesus, he brings them peace and offers them the kiss of the Spirit. The Johannine images speak of the Spirit moving deeply within the person, eliciting conversion, healing the hurts, breaking inordinate attachments, and changing us into the likeness of Jesus. It is the journey of contemplation, lovingly abiding in Christ whose power transforms from within the deepest levels of the heart. The Lukan images are more about the external signs and wonders, and the power to witness and proclaim the Good News. Both dimensions are necessary. Those who are comfortable with John alone, may need a dose of Luke. Otherwise they could be tempted to stay in the upper room enjoying intimacy with Jesus, without moving out to proclaim the Good News. They could miss out on joining with Jesus in vocalizing in the Spirit his joyful blessing prayer to the Father (Lk 10:21). Those who settle for Luke alone, may well need to grow in contemplative experience. Otherwise they will remain shallow, and not allow the deeper work of conversion to happen in their lives. Without contemplation the experience of the baptism in the Spirit does not fully blossom as intended by God.

11

COMMUNION IN THE SPIRIT

As you, Father, are in me, and I in you, may they also be one in us, so that the world may believe that you have sent me (Jn 17:21).

From all eternity within the Trinity the Father is loving the Son, and the Son loving the Father. Their love is the Holy Spirit, eternally given and eternally received in mutual self-giving. The Holy Spirit then is the unity between the Father and the Son. So whenever the Spirit is active amongst human beings, he will bring unity, not division. The Holy Spirit brings us out of isolation into communion, and out of autonomy and independence into interdependence. When the Spirit is at work he binds us together, making us one, in order to fulfill the heart-prayer of Jesus to the Father at the Last Supper, "Father may they be one in us as you are in me and I am in you" (Jn 17:21).

We are relational beings. No one is an island. We are interconnected. God's characteristic way of acting is to gather us as a people. The Greek word for Church, *ekklesia*, means the *gathering* of the people of God. In John's Gospel the words of Caiphas, the high priest, are seen by the evangelist as prophetic, "It is better for one man to die for the people than for the whole nation to be destroyed." John comments, "He did not say this on his own, but being high priest that year he prophesied that Jesus was about to die for the nation, and not for the nation only, but to gather into one the dispersed children of God"

(Jn 11:51-52). Thus he reveals the purpose of the death of Jesus – *to gather into one* the scattered children of God. It is the heart of God to gather all people to himself. When the Holy Spirit is poured out he makes real and active the unifying work that Christ accomplished for our redemption. The Holy Spirit makes us one. Paul urges the community at Ephesus to "bear with one another in love, making every effort to maintain the unity of the Spirit". He continues,

> There is one body and one Spirit, just as you were called to the one hope of your calling, one Lord, one faith, one baptism, one God and father of all, who is above all and through all and in all (Eph 4:4-6).

The Spirit Builds Community

Wherever the Spirit is moving to renew the Church he is birthing new communities. Just as the first fruit of Pentecost in the Acts of the Apostles was community, so any sovereign outpouring of the Spirit will manifest in a heart desire for communion. Luke records that once the 3,000 had been converted by Peter's preaching, "They devoted themselves to the apostles' teaching, to the fellowship, to the breaking of bread and the prayers" (Acts 2:42). This text has been foundational for many of the new communities that have sprung up within the Church in our times as a result of the new Pentecost.

We were never meant to attempt to live in the Holy Spirit as "lone-rangers". In the Western world, since the Enlightenment, we have been sold the lie that true freedom is found through rugged individualism, rather than through mutual self-giving love in interdependent relationships. Most of us are tarnished with the false idea that the autonomous individual, who is answerable to no one, is the ideal human being. Yet, this doctrine is a far cry from the notion of the Body of Christ presented in Paul's letters. Paul would have found it impossible to conceive of a Christian who claimed to have a personal relationship with Jesus, but did not belong to the Body of Christ (1 Cor 12-31).

Paul's early notion of the Body of Christ was of a concrete, intimate community of brothers and sisters bonded together in love. At that stage in his journey he was not thinking of the universal Church in an institutional way, even though later in his writings this can be found more clearly. The point I am making is simply that for Paul the *modus operandi* for any Christian was to live a vibrant community life, with like-minded people who share the beliefs and values of the Kingdom of God, and are committed together in Christ for the sake of proclaiming the gospel to their contemporaries.

From Isolation to Communion

While in her teens Heather attended a youth camp conducted by a Catholic charismatic community. She was touched by the way people talked about real issues and were very caring. While she found this confronting, because it was so different from what she had previously experienced in relationships, she was attracted to people who were free to be real about their personal struggles. She wanted that freedom. She started to follow the way of Jesus. But her friendship group at school was little help. She became dismayed as she watched her friends making wrong choices in life, and felt an increasing sense of isolation. She recalls "it was like a large mass of ice breaking up, and all the pieces floating off, leaving me by myself on a lonely piece of ice in a big sea". She wanted to live the way of Jesus, but it seemed impossible. She felt that she would inevitably have to go the way of her friends. However, at a youth gathering she heard a talk about the Holy Spirit being the power we need in our lives. She knew that was what she wanted. She decided to commit her life to Jesus as Lord, and she asked people to pray over her for the outpouring of the Holy Spirit. Now she found a new power to change, a new freedom from inner areas of sin, a new intimacy with Jesus, and an insatiable thirst for prayerful reading of the Bible.

Having a deep gratitude for the Lord's commitment to her, Heather felt called to live a committed life for the Lord in return. Coming into adulthood she thought about consecrated life, but since she desired marriage, she decided to join the predominantly lay charismatic community which had been instrumental in her conversion. In her young adult years Heather found it invaluable to be bonded with other singles who were committed to living the gospel faithfully. She was grateful to be with people who were free to share about their weaknesses and failings, and provide support for one another amidst the challenges of living and working in a social environment which was empty of God and often hostile to Christian values. She says the friendships she formed at that time in her life have endured. The inevitable conflicts that occur in friendships did not mean splitting apart and going separate ways. "In the community we were committed to working through the issues according to gospel principles of forgiveness and reconciliation." She says that without the community support and challenge it would have been almost impossible for them to remain faithful to their commitment to Jesus, and to live the moral life according to the Church's teaching. "Having others in close relationship, who can challenge us when we may be missing the mark, or wandering aimlessly down dangerous pathways, is invaluable, especially in the early years of Christian discipleship."

Now that she is married with children Heather is grateful that her children are growing up in an environment where there is a celebration of true Christian values and beliefs. Even though Heather is acutely aware of the negative influences of the secularized culture upon her children, she is not afraid. She doesn't have to be over protective of the children, since the community provides a peer group for them which off-sets the more destructive forces from the culture at large. She is confident that we can engage the world today with the gospel message. Heather and her husband have become politically active, especially in defence of human life, and she is grateful that they are not alone in this, but have others who will support them with prayer and encouragement.

Charisms for the community

It is not my intention here to present an ecclesiology, since our focus is on the way the Spirit moves in the life of the individual. It is sufficient to emphasize that any Christian who is not part of a living faith community is like a fish out of water. A "culture of Pentecost" will surely be one that brings us together, rather than isolates people into competitive pockets of self-generated ministries. In the chapter on the charisms we saw that each part of the Body is vital for the whole body. As Paul says,

> The eye cannot say to the hand, 'I have no need of you'. If a blow is being made to the eyes, the hand instinctively comes to the rescue. Neither can the hand say to the eye, 'I have no need of you'. Otherwise the hand, without eyes, will find itself in dangerous places.

Paul declares, "Now you together are the body of Christ, and individually members of it" (1 Cor 12:27). Together we make up the body of Christ, and every individual finds his or her identity through being grafted on to the body at Baptism. To be baptized in the Spirit is to be taken into deeper levels of awareness of this truth.

When Paul wrote to the Corinthians, his most overtly charismatic community, he chided them for their divisions, urging them to "be united in the same mind and the same purpose". He was well aware that some were saying, "I am for Paul", or "I am for Apollos", or "I am for Cephas" or "I am for Christ" (1 Cor 1:11-13). Competitiveness, rivalry and jealousies had led to factions and infighting. This was a clear sign that the Holy Spirit was being grieved. While affirming the spiritual charisms he stressed that they will only achieve their purpose of building the community and its mission if they are exercised with self-sacrificing love.

In Philippians Paul was addressing a similar situation. He urges the community: "Be of the same mind, having the same love, being in full accord and of one mind. Do nothing from selfish ambition or conceit, but in humility regard the other as better than yourselves. Let each of you look not to your own interests, but to the interests of others" (Phil 1:2-4). He then gives the example of Jesus, who emptied himself by becoming one of us and going further by dying on the Cross for us. True community will be built through the self-emptying of its members as they serve one another in humility, and this will bring lasting joy to the community. To be in communion is to have this mind of Christ which is always given for the other.

Pentecost and Babel

In the Acts of the Apostles, Luke draws a contrast between what was experienced on the day of Pentecost and what happened at Babel. Pentecost was the undoing of what had resulted from Babel. The Genesis account of the building of the tower of Babel begins with the people of the earth having one language, but ends with the people being divided with many languages. In contrast, the account of Pentecost begins with the people having many different languages, but ends with them being united, because each one hears the apostles speaking in their own language. While the original sin of Babel brought separation, alienation, and division, the event of Pentecost brought unity, reconciliation, and communion. The people of Babel had set out to build their tower to the heavens saying, "Come, let us build ourselves a city, and a tower with its top in the heavens, and let us make a name for ourselves; otherwise we shall be scattered abroad upon the face of the whole earth" (Gen 11:7). This was an act of pride and rebellion. The temple they were building was probably to God, but it was not *for* God. It was to "make a name for themselves"; it was for their own glory. It was the basic sin of impiety, which Paul says, left humanity under the wrath of God (Rom 1:18). Thus, having tried to take a position of strength against God they were scattered and alienated from one another.

At Pentecost with the outpouring of the Spirit this situation was reversed. Now by the action of the Spirit a new city and a new temple can be built, a civilization of love, where the thrust is towards humility, obedience and self-sacrificing love. The apostles were not trying to usurp the role of God, but rather, the people who heard them testified, "In our own languages we hear them speaking about God's deeds of power" (Acts 2:11). The apostles were not glorifying themselves but were proclaiming the great works of God. It is *God's* power, not human ingenuity that will build a true community, which will be a sign and instrument of a unified humanity.

Where the Spirit is present relationships are healed and reconciliation occurs. Paul says, "All this is from God who reconciled us to himself through Christ, and has given us the ministry of reconciliation; that is, in Christ God was reconciling the world to himself ... so we are ambassadors for Christ, since God is making his appeal through us; we entreat you on behalf of Christ, be reconciled to God" (2 Cor 5:18-20). The experience of communion in the Spirit brings us into a whole new way of relating with one another, which is different from the world's way. Communion in Christ brings us into the experience of the warmth of the Father's love. The affection of brothers and sisters mediates to us a deep sense of the Father's care and fidelity. This heals the wound of rejection, so often found within the hearts of people today, restoring us to a healthy vision of self, of others, and of God himself.

Communion in the Spirit is a way towards holiness. In committed relationship with one another we allow our lives to be intertwined in bonds of love. We learn how to forgive and to resolve conflicts, moving towards genuine reconciliation. We learn to be accountable to one another, and also to respect the intrinsic dignity of each person, holding each one as precious gold. The Holy Spirit teaches us in his "school of love". Without the nurture and challenge of community life of one kind or another it is hard to see how we could really learn to love and grow in humility, thus being changed into the likeness of Jesus.

Community: Strength in Crisis

Betty and Jim have been married for twenty years and are grateful for belonging to an intentional Catholic charismatic community, which they each joined before they were married. Jim came from a Uniting Church background. As a young man he experienced a new outpouring of the Holy Spirit at a Church camp. This sent him on a search for a spiritual home. A friend invited him to Mass which included charismatic style of worship. While his first entry into a Catholic church was full of trepidation, he says, "As soon as I walked in the door I knew I was home." He felt he could flow with the flavour of worship, but also he felt immediately the drawing of the Eucharist. He quickly accepted the invitation to relate within the community, where he found solid Catholic teaching, and developed a deep love and appreciation of the Church. Most of all he was convicted beyond doubt of the truth of the Eucharist, and its centrality in our lives. He soon joyfully entered into full communion with the Catholic Church.

Betty grew up a Catholic, and as a teenager experienced the baptism in the Spirit through a local youth ministry, which was conducted by the same charismatic community. She says the release of the Spirit made the liturgy come alive. She also was drawn to the community life, since at community gatherings the worship, teachings, and prophecies spoke powerfully to her. She knew she needed this context to be able to grow strong in her Catholic faith.

Both Jim and Betty testify that belonging to an intentional community which has regular gatherings, small groups for sharing and fellowship, and teaching on faith and morals, has kept them focused on Christ, and helped them deepen in their Catholic identity. In times of crisis they have felt deeply supported by members of the community. When Jim and two of their children were involved in a serious car accident, Betty felt that "the community was holding me up", both in prayer and practical help. When their marriage hit a major crisis, and worldly advice was for them to separate, since it seemed an irretrievable situation, they were able to hang in with one another and work it through. They are sure that without the context and support of the community around them they would not have made it through the crisis. Because of the relationships of trust and commitment, friends in the community were able to speak the truth in love to them, supporting and challenging them to battle through. They are also grateful that in the community they have received good formation on the sacramental nature of marriage, and that through the Holy Spirit they can draw upon God's power to sustain their marriage. Not that they claim miracles, but they have certainly known the power of the sacrament, which has given them the grace not to give up in the tough times.

Betty and Jim say they are constantly challenged within the community to participate in the mission of Jesus. This is important for their primary mission as a couple in rearing their children. But they also encourage and support one another in their individual vocations as a teacher and scientist, and they enjoy the opportunities that arise to go on mission together, even in cross-cultural situations. Their individual lives and their life together witness to the genuine fruit of the new Pentecost in communion of love for the sake of others.

12

FIRE TO EVANGELIZE

Make the preaching of the Good News your life's work, in thoroughgoing service (2 Tim 4:5).

Proclaiming the Gospel

The Holy Spirit gives us a new fire to proclaim the Good News. The "big grace" of experiencing a personal Pentecost in our lives sets us on fire to share the love of God with others. On the day of Pentecost the apostles were so filled with a new zeal and boldness that they were unstoppable in proclaiming to others the wonderful goodness of God. They received the gift of utterance; the grace of speaking in the Spirit in a compelling and persuasive way. As they spoke to the widely diverse assembly, gathered from different ethnic backgrounds, all the people understood them in their own native language. The people were astounded: "In our own languages we hear them speaking about God's deeds of power" (Acts 2:11). Then Peter stood up, raised his voice and began to preach. This was not a sermon to titillate the ears or to impress by eloquence. It was a fiery proclamation of the *kerygma*, the death and resurrection of Jesus, and its significance for our lives. He spoke in the power of the Holy Spirit. Pulling no punches he announced to the people "you crucified and killed Jesus of Nazareth!", but "God raised him from the dead, because it was impossible for him to be held in its power" (Acts 2:23).

We are told when they heard Peter's words "they were cut to the heart", and they said, "what must we do, brothers?" (Acts 2:37). The Holy Spirit was convincing them of the truth of the word spoken by Peter. The Holy Spirit was at work fulfilling the promise Jesus had made, that when the Advocate came he would "convince the world of sin" (Jn 16:10-11). The people understood that through their sins they had crucified Jesus, even if they personally had not been the ones to hammer the nails into his hands and his feet. So when the three thousand asked "What should we do?" Peter answered, "Repent, and be baptized in the name of Jesus Christ so that your sins may be forgiven; and you will receive the gift of the Holy Spirit" (Acts 2:38). The response was twofold, but one action overall. Firstly, they were to open their hearts through genuine sorrow for their sins, and to believe in what Christ has done for us. Secondly they were to be baptized in the name of Jesus Christ, and receive the Holy Spirit. Here it meant water Baptism by which they were saturated in the Spirit of God, sharing in the experience of Pentecost with the apostles.

The Only Name by Which We are Saved

Empowered by the Spirit of Pentecost the apostles who had previously been huddled in the upper room, unsure of their identity and afraid to obey the commission of Jesus to proclaim the gospel, now burst out of their hiding place and fearlessly shouted this Good News from rooftops. When Peter and John were hauled before the Sanhedrin to account for the healing of a crippled man, they were asked, "By what power, and by whose name have you men done this?" (Acts 4:7). The man was well known, having been crippled from birth, and every day people saw him begging at the Temple gate. Now he was "walking and jumping and praising God" and couldn't stop telling everyone that he had been healed instantly when Peter had said to him, "I have no silver or gold, but what I have I give you; in the name of Jesus Christ of Nazareth, stand up and walk!" (Acts 3:6). Before the Sanhedrin these simple fishermen from Galilee did not quiver. We are told that "filled with the Spirit" Peter began to address them. He again preached the truth. "It was by the name of Jesus Christ the Nazarene, the one you crucified, whom God raised from the dead, by this name and by no other that this man is able to stand perfectly healthy here today ... For of all the names in the world given to men, this is the only one by which we can be saved" (Acts 4:10-12).

Boldness in Proclamation

Peter preached the same kerygmatic message in the Spirit to the members of the Sanhedrin, but they were hard of heart. Pride and arrogance blocked them from the grace of repentance. But we are told, "When they saw the *boldness* of Peter and John and realized that they were uneducated and ordinary men, they were amazed and recognized them as companions of Jesus" (Acts 4:13). The members of the Sanhedrin were bewildered by the transformation that had taken place in these common Galilean fisherman. It was beyond explanation. This new *boldness* came from the Holy Spirit. The word in Greek for boldness is *parresia,* which has its derivation in the ancient Greek state, where democracy began. It meant that all Greek citizens knew they had the right to speak in the marketplace, and the right to be heard. When it was used in the New Testament, it meant that the citizens of the Kingdom of God knew that they had a right to speak the Good News of Jesus Christ and a right to be heard. Even when the Sanhedrin tried to gag Peter and John from speaking again in the name of Jesus, they replied fearlessly, "We cannot but speak of what we have seen and heard ... we must obey God rather than men" (Acts 4:20; 5:29). Even after they had been flogged, they considered it a privilege to have suffered humiliation for the name of Jesus (Acts 5:41). Nothing on this earth was going to stop them giving witness to the Good News of Jesus Christ.

Before ascending to the Father, Jesus had promised, "You will receive power when the Holy Spirit has come upon you; and you will be my witnesses in Jerusalem, in all Judea and Samaria, and to the ends of the earth" (Acts 1:8). These words must have been ringing in the ears of the apostles as they exploded into mission. The promise of the power of the Spirit gave them assurance that when they stood up for Jesus and spoke in his name, Jesus would stand up with them, and bring power to their words. The Holy Spirit is the "principal agent of evangelization".[72] The Holy Spirit brings fire to the preacher. One famous preacher, John Wesley, used to say of his technique, "I set myself on fire by the Spirit; then by my words I let others catch the fire."

The Holy Spirit also gives the words to be spoken. Jesus warned his disciples, "You will be dragged before governors and kings for my sake, to bear witness before them and the pagans." But he assured them, "do not worry about how you are to speak or what you are to say; for what you are to say will be given to you at that time; for it is not you who speak, but the Spirit of your Father speaking through you" (Mt 10:19-20). The Holy Spirit gives the gift of utterance, bringing forward the message most appropriate for the listeners. An example of this is St Anthony of Padua, one of the foremost Franciscan preachers, whose words converted thousands and were often accompanied by signs and wonders. He says,

> The apostles for their part spoke as the Holy Spirit gave them utterance. Blessed is he who speaks under the inspiration of the Holy Spirit and not as his own human spirit suggests. There are some who speak from their own spirit: they pilfer the words of others and pass them off as their own, taking the credit to themselves. ... Let us speak then as the Holy Spirit gives us utterance. Let us ask him humbly and earnestly to bestow the grace on us, so that we may fulfill the day of

Pentecost ... Let us ask for a keen sentiment of contrition, and for fiery tongues to profess the true faith ...[73]

The Anointing of the Spirit

The word "Christian" means the "anointed one". Through Baptism and Confirmation we have been anointed with the oil of chrism. We have been made "other Christs". In the Old Testament priests, prophets and kings were anointed with oil as a sign of their authority and the favour of God upon them. In fulfillment of this Old Testament figure, Jesus was anointed with the Holy Spirit. He is the Messiah, the Christ, the Anointed One. When the apostle Peter was preaching in the house of Cornelius he said, "God anointed Jesus of Nazareth with the Holy Spirit and power" (Acts 10:38). This is a reference to his baptism in the Jordan, when the Spirit came upon Jesus to anoint him and to empower him for mission. When Jesus stood in the synagogue at Nazareth, and read from the prophet Isaiah, applying the text to himself, he proclaimed, "The Spirit of the Lord is upon me. He has anointed me and sent me to bring the Good News to the poor" (Lk 4:18).

This anointing of the Spirit upon Jesus is meant for us as well. As the Holy Spirit came upon Jesus in the Jordan, confirming him as "the Christ", the Anointed One, so the Holy Spirit came down upon the apostles and Mary at Pentecost, making them to be the "anointed ones" of God, sharing in all the blessings of Christ. The fullness of the Spirit is found in Jesus, and he "gives the Spirit without measure" (Jn 3:34). "From his fullness we have all received, grace upon grace" (Jn 1:16). The Church is brought about by the Spirit of Christ, by sharing in Christ's anointing. We are Christ's body, animated by the Spirit, a messianic people. We are an anointed people, consecrated with the Spirit, for the mission of Christ. Through the anointing with the oil of chrism at Baptism and Confirmation we share in the anointing of Jesus. This anointing is for mission.

However, our sacramental anointing can be "tied up", restrained, and ineffectual in our lives.[74] We can live as if we have no anointing. The sacramental anointing we have received is meant to have a transformative effect on our lives. We have been anointed, consecrated *for mission*. When we seek to proclaim the word, we are not meant to move in our own strength, or by our own lights, or by our own eloquence, but rather under the anointing of the Spirit. We need to know who we are, the anointed ones of God.

Moving Under the Anointing of the Spirit

When we are moving under the anointing of the Spirit we are aware of the presence of God in an almost tangible way. What we speak does not just come from us; what we sing is not just produced by our own skills; when we reach out in love to others it is not just coming from ourselves. The anointing of the Spirit can come powerfully upon a time of worship, or on an inspired preaching, or on a moment when praying with another, or on a healing service, indeed on any situation where we are in prayer or mission. When the anointing is manifest there is something *more* happening which cannot be accounted for by ordinary, natural investigation. This "more" factor, the mysterious anointing of the Spirit, makes all the difference. When Peter stood up to preach on the day of Pentecost, he was moving under the anointing. That brought the power to elicit genuine conversion. In today's Church we need the same. As one African bishop said, "Peter preached one sermon and 3,000 were converted; we preach 3,000 sermons and not one person is converted." The difference is in the anointing. We must pray for the anointing. We must open ourselves to the anointing. We must move humbly under the anointing.

Maybe the anointing we have received through Baptism and Confirmation is still, as it were, packaged in a bottle, and needs to be set free. When Mary of Bethany came to anoint Jesus she had an alabaster jar full of expensive ointment, worth one year's wages. She extravagantly broke the jar and let the ointment fall on the body of Jesus (Jn 12:1-8). This was a sign that the body of Jesus, the Anointed One, would be broken on the Cross, and from his heart, broken open for us, would flow the living water of the Spirit. From his wounded side the church would be anointed. The alabaster jar represents our humanity. We need to be broken with Jesus on the Cross so the anointing can be released. We need to have all our pride and arrogance broken so the anointing can be fully manifest in our lives.

Taking this further, we should emphasize that moving under the anointing of the Spirit is not just an occasional reality, when we are engaged in Spirit-filled ministry. It is rather a state of being. Paul says we are "the aroma of Christ". Wherever we go people should be touched by the "sweet smell" of our lives (2 Cor 2:14). Knowing who we are, the anointed ones of God, we can become *more fully* who we are. John says that since we are "anointed by the Holy One" we have knowledge, and if we have not lost the anointing then the Holy Spirit will teach us everything (1 Jn 2:20, 27). If we have been consistently *living* under the anointing of the Spirit, we can confidently call upon the anointing to make any ministry effective for the Kingdom.

Crazy for Jesus

Barry cannot remember much about his Confirmation. He chose Luke for his name, because of Luke Skywalker. At the time the ritual meant nothing to Barry. But now he knows that when hands were laid on him and he was anointed with the holy chrism by the Bishop, he was given "power from on high" to be a witness to Jesus. Arriving in the big city from a country town at the age of 18 he felt totally alone and lost. He was missing family and friends and couldn't work out the purpose for his life. One night he cried out to God, "If you are real, show me." Even making the prayer brought him peace. A couple of days later a friend rang up to invite him to a youth camp. There he heard the simple gospel message for the first time. He responded and asked to be prayed over for the Holy Spirit. He felt soaked in love, and began to experience healing of past hurts, especially in family relationships. Sometime later at a charismatic Mass the priest challenged the congregation that if anyone present had never stood publicly for Jesus then to do so now. Barry stood up, and was prayed over. He just wanted to do what God wanted for him. This was the beginning of his new ministry of proclamation. The personal knowledge of God's love healed his poor self-image and gave him a strong sense of his worth and dignity.

With this new security in his identity in the Lord, he felt that the love of God within him could not be contained. He felt compelled to speak to others about his new found joy. "I had a new freedom, a new self-confidence, a new courage to share my faith. I was on fire with God's love. I just wanted everyone to know this overflowing love of God." Barry joined a group of young Catholics who would venture into the inner city at lunch time and sing songs, and talk to people about Jesus. He had become "crazy for Jesus". This anointing of the Spirit to stand up for Jesus, and to speak boldly the gospel message, has continued in Barry's life. He knows that whenever he stands up to preach, whether it is at conference, or in a church, or in an informal setting in someone's home, he is not alone. Jesus stands up with him.

The Kerygma and Conversion

While the message proclaimed will vary immensely through the creativity of the Holy Spirit adapting the word to the immediate situation and particular needs of the listeners, it will always be *kerygmatic*.[75] By this we mean that it will proclaim the vital significance of the death and resurrection of Jesus. The Spirit convinces the preacher first of the truth of what Jesus has accomplished on the Cross for our sake, and how our hope is in his glorious resurrection. This is the fire that has come to the earth, for which Jesus longed (Lk 12:49). It is what the Greeks were seeking, without knowing it, when they came to Phillip and begged, "We want to see Jesus!" (Jn 12:22). The preacher in the Spirit seeks to bring this fire to the hearts of those who hear the word. The *kerygma* contains the kernel of the message. Proclaimed in the Spirit the *kerygma* births faith, and gives rebirth to those whose faith has become complacent and diminished. As Paul reminded the Corinthians, "During my stay with you, the only knowledge I claimed to have was about Jesus, and only about him as the crucified Christ" (1 Cor 2:2). He said that he wasn't relying on rhetoric, eloquence or philosophical arguments, "only a demonstration of the power of the Holy Spirit" (1 Cor 2:5).

The Holy Spirit also awakens conversion in the heart of those who hear the word. When the gospel is proclaimed in the Spirit there is a power which opens the listener's heart. We are told that when Paul proclaimed the word to Lydia, "the Lord opened her heart to accept what Paul was saying" (Acts 16:15). There is an intrinsic power in the gospel, when it is proclaimed in the Spirit, to awaken hearts to conversion. Pope Paul VI taught, "The Church evangelizes when she seeks to convert solely through the Divine power of the message she proclaims."[76] Similarly Pope John Paul II insisted, "The proclamation of the word of God has Christian conversion as its aim:

a complete and sincere adherence to Christ and his gospel through faith ... accepting by a personal decision that Jesus is Lord ..."[77] The Spirit acts to bring *metanoia*, a change of heart, an interior revolution, through a turning away from sin and a turning to Christ as our Lord and Saviour.

Signs and Wonders

When word of God is proclaimed the Holy Spirit witnesses to the truth of Jesus by signs and wonders. Jesus pointed to his miracles as proof of his identity as the Messiah. When John the Baptist's disciples ask him whether he was the one they had been expecting, he says, "Go and tell John what you see and hear: the blind receive their sight, the lame walk, the lepers are cleansed, the deaf hear, the dead are raised to life" (Mt 11:5). In the Acts of the Apostles, Peter describes Jesus as a man "attested...by God with deeds of power, wonders, and signs that God did through him" (Acts 2:22). Later Peter witnesses in Cornelius' household that Jesus "went about doing good and healing all who were oppressed by the devil" because "God anointed Jesus of Nazareth with the Holy Spirit and with power" (Acts 10:38).

The Acts of the Apostles gives testimony to many marvels and wonders performed by the Spirit of Jesus. They were all worked in the name of Jesus, through the power of the Spirit. They were never done in the name of any individual or anyone's authority other than Jesus. The early Christians understood that the ministry of the Church in the power of the Spirit was a continuation of the ministry of Jesus. What had been manifest in Jesus' proclamation of the gospel, they expected in the Church's proclamation also. As Mark tells us, "they went out and proclaimed the good news everywhere, while the Lord worked with them and confirmed the message by the signs that accompanied it" (Mk 16:20).

Why should it be any different today? Faith is the issue. With a new release of the Holy Spirit in our lives we can move from having only believing and trusting faith to also having *expectant* faith. We can see the shift in Martha when she was grieving the death of Lazarus her brother. Jesus had arrived late. Although Martha believed that if Jesus had arrived earlier he could have saved Lazarus from dying, when he says to her, "Your brother will rise again," she responds with an act of faith in the doctrine of the resurrection on the last day. Jesus then takes her further, to an act of faith in him personally as the Christ. But when he asks them to roll back the stone, she hesitates, "Lord, by now he will smell; this is the fourth day." Jesus replies, "Have I not told you that if you believe you will see the glory of God" (Jn 11:39-40). He is calling for *expectant* faith, which goes beyond believing in doctrine, and trusting in his love. It is a "faith that moves mountains". They rolled away the stone; and the rest is history. The Lord wants his glory to be shown, but he calls for faith.

Why would the Lord want miracles to occur? Miracles upset the wisdom of the wise. They confound human wisdom and science, which wants to be able to explain everything by its own laws. More so they are a sign to the unbeliever, drawing us to greater faith. As signs they are meant to attract us to the one signified, to take us to the feet of Jesus in faith, gratitude and adoration. They are meant to build up the faith. However, they are never meant to be ends in themselves. Jesus warns against those who demand "signs and wonders" as a condition for believing. He complains, "Unless you see signs and wonders you will not believe" (Jn 4:48). When he denounces this wicked generation that demands signs and wonders, he says the only sign they will be given is the sign of Jonah i.e. the call to repentance. Chasing the signs and wonders, stuck in the excitement of the benefit they bring, is religion gone wrong because it is greedy and self-centred. On the other hand, to dismiss the possibility of miracles is an act of arrogance towards God and refusal to bow before his Almighty power.

The Process of Evangelization

So far we have been reflecting on the proclamation of the word in the power of the Spirit. This is a key moment in a whole process of evangelization. I have started with this aspect of evangelization since it is the one given most priority by the papal teaching in recent times. The papal documents consistently emphasize the priority of direct proclamation of the word. Writing to the laity John Paul II insisted, "The 'good news' is directed to stirring a person to conversion of heart and life and a clinging to Jesus Christ as Lord and Saviour; to disposing a person to receive Baptism and the Eucharist and to strengthen a person in the prospect and realization of new life according to the Spirit."[78]

Pope Paul VI stated emphatically that "evangelizing is in fact the grace and vocation proper to the Church, her deepest identity. She exists in order to evangelize ..."[79] Pope John Paul II stressed that "the call to mission derives, of its nature, from the call to holiness ... The universal call to holiness is closely linked to the universal call to mission. Every member of the faithful is called to holiness and mission."[80] And most emphatically he pronounced, "I sense that the moment has come to commit all of the Church's energies to a new evangelization and to the mission *ad gentes*. No believer in Christ, no institution of the Church can avoid this supreme duty: to proclaim Christ to all peoples."[81]

While keeping our focus on the need for proclamation, we now need to look at the *full dynamic process* of the evangelizing work of the Church. Firstly, we are called to *witness* through our individual lives and through the life of the Christian community. Through this wordless witness we stir up irresistible questions in the hearts of those who see how we live. People today put more trust in witnesses than in teachers, and if they do trust teachers it will be because of the credibility of their witness.[82] Secondly, as we have seen, we are called to *proclaim* the word. It is not enough to have programs welcoming people back to the parish, when there is no explicit proclamation of the gospel. As Pope Paul VI emphasized, "Evangelization will always contain – as foundation, centre, and at the same time, summit of its dynamism – clear proclamation that, in Jesus Christ, the Son of God made man, who died and rose from the dead, salvation is offered to all men and women, as a gift of God's grace and mercy."[83]

As we have already seen the goal of the proclamation is to bring people to a total *conversion*, whereby they turn from sin and decide to "accept the saving sovereignty of Christ and become his disciple."[84] For conversion, as in the other moments of the evangelizing process, we need the sovereign action of the Holy Spirit. Sometimes the Holy Spirit brings about conversion suddenly and dramatically; at other times more gradually. As we have seen the "big grace" of the baptism in the Holy Spirit is a powerful impetus for adult conversion.

The next phase in the process of evangelization is fuller *incorporation into the life of the Church*. This presumes that there already is a lively faith community into which a person can be initiated. The contemporary challenge is to develop these vibrant communities which provide a context for growth in *discipleship*. Jesus sent out his apostles to "make disciples" (Mt 28:19). The challenge for the community is to find ways that those who have experienced an initial personal conversion can go forward in an on-going way deepening in their life of faith and in their understanding of the ways of God. This includes many elements such as personal prayer, love for the Scriptures, joyful participation in the sacraments, especially the Eucharist, and finding ways to serve within the community as well as engaging in apostolic works.

The final phase in the process is often overlooked. The work of evangelization is not complete until those evangelized are fully *equipped* to become evangelists. Pope Paul VI called this "the test of truth, the touchstone of evangelization". He went on to challenge all of us, "It is unthinkable that a person should accept the Word and give himself or herself to the Kingdom without becoming a person who bears witness to it and proclaims it in turn."[85] When we have received the amazing gift of the inexhaustible treasure of Christ it would be "unthinkable" to bury that treasure within ourselves and not share it with others. Paul says we are stewards of the Mystery of Christ (1 Cor 4:1; Col 1:25). A steward is someone who has been entrusted with a precious treasure by the Master. To be good stewards we must be found worthy of this trust. We must not squander this precious gift, or neglect the grace that has been given. We must be found at the work of evangelizing when the Master returns. Again the Holy Spirit is the key. When the Spirit is active within us we are urged to go beyond ourselves in sharing the Good News. The Holy Spirit stirs the apostolic fervor within us and gives us the courage to venture outside of our "comfort zone" in witnessing the love of God to others.

The New Evangelization

The phrase "new evangelization" was first coined by Pope John Paul II during his visit to Poland in 1979. He used it then without any explanation. Later in Santo Domingo speaking to the Latin American Bishops he used it more deliberately and described it as "new in ardour, in method and expression".[86] Again and again he came back to this theme. He was making a distinction between the evangelization needed in virgin missionary territory and that needed for lukewarm and de-Christianized, mainly Western, nations which were traditionally "Christian countries". The latter need a "new evangelization". He explains:

> The new evangelization does not consist of a 'new gospel' ... Neither does it involve removing from the Gospel whatever seems difficult for the modern mentality to accept ... The new evangelization has as its point of departure the certitude that in Christ there are 'inexhaustible riches' (Eph 3:8) which no culture nor era can exhaust ... These riches are, first of all, Christ himself, his person, because he himself is our salvation.[87]

The Pope was fully aware that a "new evangelization" was needed in those countries that may have been evangelized many centuries ago, and had in many ways embedded Christian beliefs and values in their culture. Under the pressure of secularization, the so-called "Christian society" in these countries has been dismantled. The majority of people in these countries have lost a lived faith, even if they are nominally Christian, and "many no longer consider themselves members of the Church, and live far removed from Christ and the gospel".[88] At the beginning of the third millennium the Pope, looking back on his long pontificate, and seeking to guide the Church into the future, stated,

> Over the years, I have often repeated the summons to the new evangelization. I do so again now, especially in order to insist that we must rekindle in ourselves the impetus of the beginnings and allow ourselves to be filled with the ardour of the apostolic preaching which followed Pentecost. We must revive in ourselves the burning conviction of Paul, who cried out: "Woe to me if I do not preach the Gospel (1 Cor 9:16).[89]

The new evangelization is the Church seeking to reclaim its true identity in the world today. It is the Church responding to the weakened faith and the confusion in the moral lives of our contemporaries. Many of the baptized live in a world indifferent or hostile towards God. Many live in a sort of practical atheism. The Church is seeking to find a new way to proclaim the gospel in this context.

At the turn of the century Pope John Paul II set out for us the new agenda for the Church. It is quite simply to seek the face of Christ. More than anything the new evangelization seeks to proclaim Christ. In all of his teachings Pope John Paul II was adamant that Christianity is not in any conventional sense a religion. It is an experience of encounter with Jesus Christ crucified and risen. It is about being captured by the amazing love of Christ who died for us and is now risen. If we open our hearts to Christ then we will discover our true humanity. That is why he calls us back to Pentecost. Here is where we will find the fire for the new evangelization. A new Pentecost experience in the life of every Catholic will transform the world. We need to be filled again with the ardor of the apostolic preaching at Pentecost. We need again the burning conviction of St Paul who professes, "All I want is to know Jesus Christ, and the power of his resurrection" (Phil 3: 10). He lived and died proclaiming the gospel: "For it is not ourselves that we are preaching, but Christ Jesus as the Lord, and we are your servants for Jesus' sake. It is the same God who said, 'Let there be light shining out of darkness', who has shone in our minds to radiate the light of the knowledge of God's glory, the glory on the face of Christ" (2 Cor 4:5-6).

Release of the Charisms

The new evangelization will be marked by a new creativity from the Holy Spirit. We can desire and expect a new effusion of the spiritual gifts for the sake of the proclamation of the gospel. Under the anointing of the Holy Spirit Jesus freely exercised charisms in his ministry of the word and in his ministry of healing and deliverance from demons. He then sent out his apostles to proclaim the Good News, and to heal and cast out demons (Lk 9:1). In the early Church as reported in the Acts of the Apostles and the epistles of Paul, the charisms were manifest both in the ministry of the word and the ministry of healing, which always accompanied the word. There are many spiritual gifts that serve the work of evangelization. Those gifts most geared towards evangelization can be roughly grouped into two clusters, developed around this twofold ministry of Jesus and his Church. Firstly, associated with the ministry of the word are many wonderful charisms. The gift of wisdom, granting insight that helps breakthrough with problems and making decisions; the gift of knowledge giving intuitive understanding of a truth of the faith; the gifts of preaching and teaching; the gift of prophecy by which a person becomes a channel of God's word for a group or for individuals; the gift of being an evangelist, which is an extraordinary grace empowering the sharing of the Good News, above the normal duty that all Christians have to evangelize; the gift of being a missionary, which empowers us to feel free to bring the Good News in another culture.

Associated more with the ministry of healing and deliverance we find another exciting list of charisms. We have already spoken of the gift of healing itself, which is in these days becoming important to help people find an opening to God. Their lives are often so bruised and broken that without the healing touch of the Lord they are unable to comprehend the love of God. Along with healing are those gifts such as the gift of encouragement, being empowered to comfort and counsel others in an affirming way; also the gift of discernment of spirits, which helps to perceive quickly the activity of evil spirits, and also pick up on an intense presence of God; the gift of hospitality, which empowers us to be welcoming and embracing of others in need; the gift of faith, which expects God to act in extraordinary ways, and the gift of working miracles in a such a way that the Spirit draws the unbeliever.

Opening our lives to the infilling of the Holy Spirit, we find that the Holy Spirit himself equips us for the work of evangelization. The distribution of his gifts is a significant way that he does this. If we are open to receiving the gifts, and discern well our primary gifting, we can be so much more useful for the Lord in fulfilling his purpose of bringing many people into living relationship with him and his Church.

Empowered for Mission

Jenny had been puzzled when, as a young mother, she had a number of unexplainable spiritual experiences. She had sought the advice of priests and religious, but had not found anyone who she felt understood her. Then while at a school sacramental preparation meeting she met another mother with whom she felt free to confide. At last she felt someone understood what was happening to her. This new friend invited her to a prayer meeting, and offered to pray with her. Jenny was hesitant because her friend had told her that the Holy Spirit would change her life. She wasn't sure she wanted to change. However, she began to pray for a sign from the Lord that it was his will for her to be prayed over for the Holy Spirit. A few days later an old Christian friend, whom she had not seen for years, rang out of the blue, just to tell her that God had put Jenny on her heart and she was praying for her. Jenny saw this as a sign from the Lord. So she made a time to receive prayer for the baptism in the Spirit. As she was prayed over she felt the power of the Holy Spirit come upon her so powerfully that she couldn't move. Yet she didn't feel trapped or bound up. She just felt totally helpless under the power of the Spirit. She could not stop praising God with immense joy and freedom.

During the next few months she was awakening in the Spirit, finding herself with a new love and sensitivity for the plight of others. She found herself changing from being a "people pleaser" to being her own self, not afraid of what others thought of her. She says, "I moved from not knowing who I was to knowing I was a daughter of God. My identity was not simply being a wife of someone, a mother of someone. I was opening up to being my true self. I came alive." Inner healing helped with this, as she allowed the Spirit to surface the hurts of the past. As a little girl she had suffered under an alcoholic and abusive father, and then had gone on to marry an alcoholic, who had become cruel and abusive to the children. The Lord was now doing the divine surgery she needed to repair her broken heart. Now she was more herself Jenny experienced a call to love others, to go beyond caring for her own needs, and to begin to share the goodness of God with those who do not know his love.

One night while praying at home Jenny saw a figure of Jesus before her which evoked fear and awe. He was beckoning her with his finger, saying, "Follow me." She interpreted this as a call to ministry. Another night, as she woke up, she again saw Jesus, and heard him say to her, "I want you to lead my people." But how could a forty-year-old mother of five, who had an alcoholic husband, be meant to fulfill this calling?

Jenny relates that the children saw the difference immediately. There had been a major change in her mothering, and they were delighted. But the Lord also began to create opportunities for Jenny to become equipped for mission beyond the family in the local church. Out of the blue she was invited to do a leadership training course, and then afterwards a school of evangelization. Then she was offered to do a Spiritual Direction course, and a Prayer Leaders course. Jenny was being equipped for mission. She became a significant spiritual leader of other women. Under the new grace she had received Jenny was influencing the lives of many people, and leading them to encounter the Lord. When in her late forties it was no longer tenable for her husband to stay with her due to cruelty and abuse, Jenny returned to the workforce, landing a job at a prominent university, and then later at a major Catholic hospital. She was invited to do a chaplaincy course and to join the pastoral care team at the hospital. Now she is the Director of Mission at the hospital. She shares the love in the heart of Jesus with whoever she meets. The release of the power of the Spirit in Jenny's life empowered her to use her gifts and to be the sweet fragrance of the "aroma of Christ" in the lives of many.

Need for Intercession

One charism that has not been mentioned is that of intercession. Some people have a special gift in this area, happily devoting much time crying out for others, and being the means of God's grace falling upon their lives. Whether we have the special charism or not, all evangelization needs to be undergirded by prayer. Paul begs the help of prayer for his work: "I beg you by our Lord Jesus Christ and the love of the Spirit, to help me through my dangers by praying to God for me" (Rom 16:30). He himself laboured in prayer even for those he had not yet met, offering his suffering on their behalf. To the Colossians he wrote, "I want you to know that I do have to struggle hard for you ... and for so many others who have never seen me face to face" (Col 2:1). And he reports to the Colossians how one of their own is praying for them: "Epaphras, your fellow citizen, sends his greetings; this servant of Christ Jesus never stops battling for you.

Praying that you will never lapse but always hold perfectly to the will of God" (Col 4:12). In the work of God we are always in the midst of a battle and need constant prayer.

A classic biblical image for this battle of prayer is Moses on the mountain when the Israelites were fighting the Amalekites on the plain below. As long as Moses kept his arms raised in prayer the advantage in the battle went to the Israelites; but if he lowered his arms through tiredness the advantage went to the Amalekites. To assist him Aaron and Hur took up post on either side holding up his arms, so he could remain in continuous prayer (Ex 17:8-16).

Overcoming Strongholds of Darkness

We can forget how crucial it is to have the prayer warriors at work when we are evangelizing. Earlier we spoke about the activity of evil spirits in the world. Now is time to speak about another away Satan and evil spirits seek to undo the work of God. They seek to oppose the proclamation of the gospel and are determined to maintain the strongholds they have gained in those who have not yet come to the light of faith, or are in some way influenced by powers of evil. Intercessory prayer is very effective in breaking the power of these strongholds and ushering in the Kingdom of Light and Love. We are assured by Jesus that "the gates of hell will not prevail" against the Church (Mt 16:18). This does not meant that somehow we will just limp into the Kingdom after being beaten around and mauled by evil spirits. Rather, it means that when the gospel is proclaimed the strongholds of darkness will not be able to resist. This is especially the case if the proclamation is accompanied by persistent prayer. Catherine of Siena used to urge her friends to stand at the foot of the Cross of Jesus and as it were collect the blood that he shed there for sinners. Then cast the blood of Jesus on the hardened hearts of those for whom they intercede. Even though the hearts of those for whom we pray may be as hard as diamonds, the blood of Jesus, through the means of intercession, will crack open their hearts to receive the Good News.

Asking with Confidence

We may ask the question, "Why do we have to pray; after all God knows our needs already?" By the mystery of God's loving and redeeming work in this world he has chosen to act through human instrumentality. Christ is himself the unique Mediator between God and humanity. He is continually interceding before the Father for us (Heb 7:25). All power is available to us, but he waits upon us to intercede. He is a loving Father who desires to pour his gifts upon us, but he wants us to acknowledge our weakness and dependency upon him, and to cry out to him in our need. He wants us to beseech him confidently, standing on his promises. "Whatever you ask for in my name I will do …" (Jn 14:13) and again, "If you remain in me, and my words remain in you, you may ask what you will and you will get it" (Jn 15:7). We must have expectant faith, to beg the Father with the security of a child who knows he or she is perfectly loved: "Ask and you will receive, seek and you will find, knock and the door will be opened to you" (Lk 11:9-13). It is simply a matter of total confidence in his goodness: "Everything you ask and pray for, believe that you have it already and it will be yours" (Mk 11:24).

In addition to confidence we also need to persevere. Jesus' parables about prayer are about not giving up, but persisting even when it seems impossible. The man who would not get up when a neighbour is knocking on the door for bread will have to get up if his neighbour persists. An unjust judge who is dismissing the cries of a poor widow will finally relent if she persists in worrying him to death. That is the attitude we must have before the Lord. Never give up on him, even when he seems to delay. If he delays in answering it could be simply to expand our hearts in longing, or to make sure that when he does deliver that we do not take the gift for granted but are filled with gratitude. Think of Monica praying for the conversion of Augustine all those years. Just when she thought all had gone wrong, because Augustine decided to go to Milan, that was the very time the Spirit would finally move through St Ambrose, the Bishop of Milan, to bring about this most celebrated conversion. Behind all conversions there is a story of intercession, often hidden and unknown. A man named George Muller had prayed for seventy years every day for the conversion of his friend. George died seeing no result for his faithful prayer. However, at his funeral, as the casket was being lowered, his friend was so overwhelmed by grief that he opened his heart to God. This was the beginning of his conversion.

13

GUIDED BY THE SPIRIT

He guides me along the right path; he is true to his name (Ps 23:3).

The Holy Spirit comes to lead, guide and direct us in our journey of discipleship. Jesus is the way to the Father, but the Holy Spirit is our guide along that way. The Israelites were guided through the desert by a "bright cloud" during day and a "pillar of fire" at night. Whenever the cloud lifted from the tabernacle they broke camp and moved on. If the cloud stayed over the tabernacle they remained camped. "They set out at the command of the Lord, and at his command they pitched camp" (Num 9:18). The early Fathers saw the cloud as a symbol of the Spirit, who is the guide of all those on the way to Christ.

Jesus himself was "led by the Spirit into the wilderness" (Lk 4:1). Christians also are to be "led by the Spirit" (Gal 5:18). The Acts of the Apostles makes it clear that the Holy Spirit was guiding the Church every step of the way. The Spirit tells Peter to go to Cornelius' house, where the Holy Spirit was poured out upon the Gentiles for the first time (Acts 10:19; 11:12). When the apostles gathered in Jerusalem to make decisions about the future of the Church, they announced, "It has been decided by the Holy Spirit and by ourselves …" (Acts 15:28). When Paul and Timothy were going to preach the gospel in Asia, the Holy Spirit told them not to go. Later "the Spirit of Jesus would not allow them" to go to Bythynia. Instead the Spirit gave Paul a vision in the night making it clear they were meant to go to Macedonia, something they had not considered before (Acts 16:6-10). Both in our individual journey and as Church we are the people guided by the Spirit of God.

Conscience and the Holy Spirit

Each one of us has an in-built compass which can help us navigate our way through life and steer the ship on the course that it is meant to take. If this compass is working well, we can avoid getting ship-wrecked in the shallows or be lost on the perilous high seas of life. The Holy Spirit guides this inner compass, which we call conscience. By the prompting of the Spirit our conscience is able to make judgments between what is good and what is bad for us in any concrete situation. To change the image, our conscience is like a built-in radio receiver through which the Holy Spirit speaks. This is the inner voice of conscience which is inviolable. While every human being has a conscience, and when it is used well we can attribute its function to the working of the Spirit, this is so much more the case for a believer in Christ, who has opened oneself to the infilling of the Holy Spirit. We have the advantage of being anointed by the Spirit. And John encourages, "the anointing he gave teaches you everything" (1 Jn 2:27). The Holy Spirit of truth witnesses within us to what is good, true and beautiful, and also urges us to act in this way. By the action of the Spirit within us we can distinguish between what is sinful and what is not, what is of the flesh and what is not, what is of the mentality of the world and what is not.

Our conscience helps us to make decisions which are true to our design as human beings. We can see clearly the universal moral principles which are fundamental to our humanity. By the action of the Spirit we are empowered to make moral judgments that are true to the way God created us. This guidance of the Spirit is not only given in the innermost sanctuary of conscience. Otherwise there would be too much danger of deception or confusion. Thanks be to God we have the teaching authority of the Church, which is guaranteed to be guided by the Spirit of truth, and is an "expert in humanity". Our consciences are meant to be informed by the teaching of the Church, so our decisions can be according to the will of God. The same Holy Spirit, who witnesses to the truth through the apostolic ministry of the Church also witnesses to the truth within our hearts through our conscience.

Inspirations of the Spirit

The Holy Spirit breathes where he wills. In our daily life we need to be open to his promptings. He guides and directs us to the extent we obey his promptings. Jesus lived this way. It was with the Holy Spirit that he went into the wilderness to do battle with Satan (Lk 4:1); it was in the power of the Holy Spirit that he returned and began his ministry (Lk 4:14); it was under the anointing of the Spirit that he performed his healings, exorcisms and miracles (Lk 4:18); it was "in the Holy Spirit" that he chose and instructed his apostles (Acts 1:2); it was in the Spirit that he joyfully praised the Father (Lk 10:21); it was through the Spirit that he offered himself to the Father (Heb 9:14).

Inspirations of the Spirit are interior movements initiated by the Holy Spirit to arouse us to greater holiness of life and to stir us towards apostolic activity. The Holy Spirit is constantly at work within us. When we have been baptized in the Spirit we characteristically have a keen awareness and expectancy of the Spirit's promptings. We hearken closely to the leading of the Spirit, wanting to be faithful to the grace he brings. The more we obey the leadings of the Spirit the more teachable we become, and the more richly the Holy Spirit dwells within us and possesses us. "The Holy Spirit is given to those who obey him" (Acts 5:32). When we resist the promptings of the Spirit, our hearts harden and become immovable, no longer sensitive to his action, preferring to live according to the flesh. The Holy Spirit is constantly giving us actual graces to help us fulfill the responsibilities of the present moment. We need to be open to receiving them.

Inspirations of the Spirit are sometimes given directly, e.g., a revelatory word at prayer, or a prompting to take a journey of mercy. At other times they are indirect, given through secondary causes, e.g., listening to a homily, reading a book, observing the good example of another. Whether they are indirect or direct, the Holy Spirit is the principal author, and it is essential for our growth that we obey. Inspirations of the Spirit lead to growth in virtue in a similar way that temptations lead to sinful actions. If we say yes to inspirations, we will deepen in the particular virtue (just as when we say yes to temptation we deepen in vice). To resist inspirations of the Spirit is to frustrate the work of God within us and to prevent any real growth.

Need for Discernment

We want to obey the interior promptings of the Spirit. But a problem arises. How do we know whether the interior movements that arise within us are actually from the Holy Spirit, or maybe from the evil spirit, or simply from our own psyche? Often the origin of thoughts and desires within us is not really clear. Thus the need for discernment, the process by which we seek to detect the origin of the movements of the heart, so we can be sure we are moving in the Spirit, and not being led by the evil spirit. John Cassian encourages us to be good "money-changers".[90] Just as a money changer has a keen eye for the counterfeit coin, so also do we need to be able to detect the subtle work of the evil one. The enemy disguises himself as an "angel of light", often urging us to activities that are in themselves good, but are not appropriate for us now. The "money-changer" is able to tell what is "pure gold" and what has impurities in it. Good money-changers also weigh carefully what is before them before acting.

Discernment is the Spirit-led process by which we examine, in the light of the personal knowledge of Jesus, the interior movements of the heart. We try to ascertain which of these movements lead towards God, and the doing of his will, and which deflect us from that goal. We distinguish this grace of discernment in daily life from the more rare gift of "discernment of spirits" which is a supernatural charism enabling someone to instantly identify the presence of an evil spirit in another person or in a situation. The spiritual gift of "discernment of spirits" is highly specialized to just a few. The grace of a discerning heart is a necessity for everyone who is a disciple of Jesus.

Developing a discerning heart

There are a number of pre-requisites for developing a discerning heart. These are dispositions that we need to have if we are going to be able to discern well. All these dispositions are usually the fruit of being baptized in the Holy Spirit. Firstly, we need to be convinced of God's love for us and that he wants the best for us; and as a response to this unconditional love we have a genuine desire to do his will. Because we genuinely love the Lord, we only want to do what he wants. Secondly, we need to be abiding in Christ, having an active prayer life, and an experiential knowledge of Jesus. In this way we will have a sense of his heart. The more we abide in Jesus the more accustomed we are to his ways, and can discern what is his will. To illustrate this point a story may help.[91] A couple were celebrating their 40th wedding anniversary. The wife went with her daughter to buy a gift at the men's wear department. Her eyes fell on the rack that had fifty or more neck ties all of different colours. Her daughter said, "But how will you know which one he will like?" The mother replied, "I will know." And sure enough the one she picked brought delight to her husband. How did she know what would please him? It was the fruit of an abiding relationship for forty years. So it is with the Lord. The key to discerning what will please him is to be in intimate relationship with him. The more we know him, the more we will know what is *of* him. We will be listening to the gentle voice of the Shepherd within, able to distinguish between his voice and the voice of the stranger (Jn 10:1-5).

The third disposition is being open to whatever the Lord wants. This means that you are free of all inordinate attachments, which would hold the heart captive; whatever prevents you from being free to move as the Lord would be prompting. This requires a truly surrendered heart. You understand your life to be simply for the glory of God. Any possession you have, any person or relationship you cherish, any cause or ideal which is important to you, cannot be an end in itself. Everything must serve the one fundamental purpose of your life i.e. to give glory to God. At the end of your life, just like Jesus, you will be able to say, "Father I have glorified you here on earth, and finished the work you gave me to do" (Jn 17:4). With this attitude, when it is a matter of discerning between two goods, you are able to hold them before the Lord as if on scales held in a balance, ready to be weighed down on either side by what God wants.

A fourth disposition for a discerning heart is regularly scrutinizing the heart on a daily basis. Self-knowledge is critical for discernment. We grow in a discerning heart if we often examine what has been happening within. We call this an "examen of consciousness"[92] to distinguish it from the examination of conscience. The latter looks at sinful states, and is highly recommended. The former looks at all the movements of the heart, both good and bad, in an effort to become more aware of what is moving us, and to become more sensitive to the promptings of the Spirit. The examen only takes about fifteen minutes in a day. It involves reviewing how we have experienced the touch of God during the day, through all the people, events and circumstances, as well as in the depths of the heart, and being grateful for this. We learn to see God in all things. It also involves allowing the light of the Spirit to show us where movements within us may have originated with the evil spirit, or by the urge of the flesh or the lure of the world.

Discerning a Calling

We know that by baptism each one is called to holiness. Each of us is called to union with Christ through the Holy Spirit who is within us. But we must also realize that each one of us has a *unique* calling from God. When the Holy Spirit becomes active in our lives he makes us more aware of this distinctive vocation. The words of Blessed John Henry Newman ring true:

> I am created to do something or to be something for which no one else is created; I have a place in God's counsels, in God's world, which no one else has; whether I be rich or poor, despised or esteemed by others. God knows me and calls me by name. God has created me to do him some definite service. He has committed some work to me which he has not committed to another.[93]

The Holy Spirit leads us along the path of our unique calling from God. It is never too late to respond to his loving call. Jesus told the story of the vineyard workers who were called into work at different hours of the day, but they all receive the same wage. The lateness of the hour does not matter. What matters is that we respond to the call. No one else has to offer what you have to offer. He calls you personally by name. Only you can work in the patch of the vineyard he has allotted to you.

How do we discern the leading of the Holy Spirit into "the work" the Lord has for us in the vineyard? There are at least four major pointers that indicate to us a life-calling. Firstly, what may be called the "conspiracy of the Holy Spirit". The word conspiracy comes from the Latin, *con-spirare*, which literally means to "breath together". Usually conspiracies are with evil intent; a breathing together of malice and intrigue with a potential threat to someone. But the conspiracy of the Holy Spirit is the opposite. It is a breathing together of events and circumstances in your life which providentially points you in a particular direction. By the benefit of hindsight you can see how the hand of the Lord, the Holy Spirit, has been upon your life gently, and maybe at times not so gently, taking you in a particular pathway.

Secondly, you receive a "word from the Lord". Again and again down through Christian history men and women have been inspired by a word from Sacred Scripture, or from a preaching, or from spiritual reading, or from some other means, which convinced them of the direction they should move. This is not an extraordinary revelation. We don't necessarily expect words written in the sky, or visions in the night. Rather, the word, which we sense is from the Lord, confirms the other indicators of the way we should go. The Lord does this for us, not only to move us to where he wants us to go, but also to give us something to hang on to when we begin to doubt later the veracity of the calling. Maybe we will receive a number of such words, which recorded, become signposts for us along the way.

Thirdly, and most importantly, the Spirit gives us a deep peace of heart over an extended period of time. This peace is a sense of "rightness", a sense that this "fits" me, a sense of being "at home" in this calling. The Spirit plants in us a "God-directed desire" for this path, and awakens an excitement in us, even though there may be surface apprehensions and feelings of inadequacy. It is God who puts into us "the desire, the will and the action" (Phil 2:13).

Fourthly, we need the confirmation of wise counsel. It is important not to make one's decision without submitting it to a spiritual director. We have an almost infinite capacity for self-delusion. Consequently it is good for us to use a wise counsellor or spiritual director as a mirror in which we can come to see more clearly the attitudes and motivations of the heart that underlie our attraction to this direction or to that direction.

An Unexpected Calling

Jeremy had been a practising Catholic from childhood. While an undergraduate in science he used to pray each night, asking the Lord what he was to do with his life. Towards the end of his doctoral studies he had thought of spending some time as a lay missionary in Africa. But he realized this was incompatible with his emerging career as an astrophysicist. While finishing off his doctoral thesis, he gladly accepted an offer to do post-doctoral work at the prestigious Max Planck Institute for radio astronomy in Germany. The path ahead seemed marked out clearly for him.

That was until Jeremy was invited to a Life in the Spirit Seminar, which was conducted over a series of nights, by a youth ministry that was active on the campus. Having gone to confession and opened up a sinful area of his life with genuine contrition, Jeremy was touched by a talk on giving one's life totally to God, and receiving the Holy Spirit. Later Jeremy described what was evoked in his heart: "I wanted God, pure and simple". He made an act of surrender to the Lord, was prayed over for a new infilling of the Holy Spirit, and was released in the gift of tongues. Overcome with a new love, Jeremy fell to his knees before a large *San Damiano* cross, and was for a long time caught up in prayer. Through this experience Jeremy says, "The Lord got into the driver's seat and stuck his foot on the accelerator, and off we went." He felt a new power to overcome the besetting sin he had confessed, and all the stress and anxiety of finishing the thesis was gone. "Jesus became central to my life; Jesus came into clear focus, no longer just a generalized notion of God." Now Jeremy really wanted to do what God wanted for him in his life.

Five days after his experience of the baptism in the Spirit Jeremy went for a walk with his priest-mentor. The dream about spending some time as a missionary in Africa had come up again. But his priest friend helped him see that it was all in the mind and not a reality; after all it had been with him before, but he had taken no action in that direction. The dream probably symbolized his desire to do something radical for God. Hearing this, Jeremy concluded that he was free to go to Germany according to plan. Then towards the end of the walk his mentor made a casual reference to the priestly calling, and how God unexpectedly calls young men in that direction. Jeremy knew in a moment this was what God wanted! Prior to the baptism in the Spirit Jeremy would not have allowed himself to consider this possibility, since it ruled out a career in astrophysics which was so dear to his heart. He says, "Previously it would have been impossible for me to let go of my career, but now the Holy Spirit gave me the power to do just that." Jeremy immediately informed the university that upon graduation with the PhD he would be leaving everything to train for the priesthood. Today Jeremy is a priest, and is forever grateful for the Holy Spirit providing both the inspiration for his calling and the power to act upon it. In hindsight Jeremy can see the "conspiracy of the Holy Spirit", breathing together events and circumstances that have lead him unexpectedly to where he is today. Through his time of preparation for priesthood he never doubted his calling, since the Spirit gave him a quiet peace of soul, and a sense that this was his destiny, this was why he was born.

Making Decisions

Life is full of decisions. In the ordinary flow of our life we don't have to labour too much over discerning whether minor decisions are according to the will of God. We can trust in the Holy Spirit within us; and rely upon the habitual ways of thinking, valuing and behaving that are already in place, without becoming too worried about our motivations. Sometimes zealous neophytes, or people with a warped image of God, can become too anxious and scrupulous about little matters. In worrying too much over whether this is the Lord's will or not we can become paralyzed and lose the opportunity for doing good. It is enough to practise the examen and have a regular spiritual director, who can help us gain objectivity and correct our course if necessary.

Nevertheless, when it comes to making major decisions in our lives, such as vocational issues, or deciding between two courses of action which would significantly change the shape of our lives, we need a clear process of going about it. For example you may be drawn to lay missionary work overseas, or feel it is time to change your career, or feel called to give substantial amounts of your income to a charitable cause, or feel drawn to take up a new ministry in the parish. Or you may be making a vocational life-decision. How do you seek the leading of the Holy Spirit? St Ignatius Loyola provides us with three modes of decision-making, three ways in which we can make a Spirit-led decision.[94] Before describing them, we need to be clear that here we are not deciding between good and bad actions. That is the work of the conscience. Rather we are discerning between two good courses of action. Which is the one that is the will of God for us?

The *first mode* is when the Holy Spirit provides clarity beyond doubting. This is not all that common, but can happen to us "out of the blue". The Lord moves and attracts the will in such a way that there is a profound certitude and peace immediately, and it endures. There is a sense of new freedom and delight. It is almost like a flash of light that comes unexpectedly. The recipient experiences a secure sense of being loved by God, and a burning desire to go forward in what God is asking. An example of this would be the moment that Francis of Assisi heard read in the Church the gospel text of the disciples being sent by Jesus with no money, or haversack or spare tunic or footwear or staff. He asked the priest what it meant. "Immediately, exulting in the Holy Spirit, he cried out: 'This is what I want, this is what I seek, this is what I long to do with all my heart!'." And he did it.

If the clarity and certitude of the first mode is not present, then it is good to seek the Lord's will by the *second mode*. This is when we get in touch with the way the heart is being attracted by the Spirit. The heart is drawn to one of the options as if under the attraction of a magnet. We experience a strong pull on the heart and a desire for the heart to go that way. The way this happens is through the experience of what Ignatius calls discernment of spirits, the discerning of consolation and desolation. Ignatius described consolation as "an interior movement of the soul by which it is inflamed with love of its Creator and Lord … I call consolation every increase of faith, hope and love, and all interior joy that invites and attracts to what is heavenly and to the salvation of one's soul by filling it with peace and quiet in its Creator and Lord."[95]

If one of the options is the way the Spirit is leading us, we will experience consolation when considering this option. On the other hand, if it is not the way we are meant to go, then we will experience desolation when imagining it as our future. Ignatius described desolation as "darkness of soul, turmoil of spirit, inclination to what is low and earthly, restlessness rising from many disturbances and temptations which lead to want of faith, want of hope, want of love. The soul is wholly slothful, tepid, sad and separated, as it were, from its Creator and Lord."[96]

When one particular option is being imagined before the Lord in a prayerful manner we experience either consolation or desolation. If over a period of time consolation is the prevailing experience, then it is clear that the Lord is drawing the heart towards that option. However, it is good to hold each option before the Lord over a period of time, and sense what drops down into the heart, either a joyful desire and sense of peace, or a disturbance of heart and restless anxiety. It is also important that the discernment be accompanied by a spiritual director, who by listening can help reflect back to the person what is happening.

It is possible that the second mode doesn't provide the answer requested from the Lord. Sometimes there is not sufficient clarity and understanding for the person to confidently choose either way. In that case, Ignatius suggests *the third mode* of decision-making. This third way is more to do with the mind than the heart. However, as we have said from the beginning, it is not a cold intellectual exercise, but rather a prayerful way of submitting oneself to the Lord in fervent desire of knowing his will. This mode is best exercised when the heart is in a time of tranquility, with few emotions, negative or positive. The consideration at hand is to weigh up the pros and cons of each option, to list the advantages and the disadvantages. This should be done with a spirit of complete detachment, and with a desire to do only what will give glory to God. We should be like clay in the hands of the potter. In this attitude of surrender of heart the pros and cons are weighed as objectively as possible. Then a decision is made on the basis of which set of reasons is more convincing. Then the person is encouraged to submit everything to the Lord again and prayerfully seek confirmation that it is the right decision.

Added to this third mode Ignatius also suggests other considerations. He suggests imagining how you would advise another person of the same disposition, who came to you facing the same choice you have to face. This reflection may help to give clarity. He also suggests imagining yourself at the end of your life, at the moment of death. What choice would you have wished to make? This reflection can help us to see the shortness of life, and relativize what may now seem so important. Again he suggests considering yourself before the judgment seat of God, and see on that day how you would have wished to have chosen. This reflection invites us to have an eternal perspective, which again can give clarity. All three of these considerations can help confirm the rightness of a decision already made, or they can actually help in making the decision itself.

Finally I want to emphasize again that techniques of themselves don't give us assurance that we are hearing God's word. It is rather the inspiration of the Spirit, the voice of the Lord himself, who certainly may work through whatever methods we use, but also comes to us in his own way and in his own time. The surest way of being a Spirit-led person is to deepen in personal prayer, abiding in the love of Christ, and growing in familiarity with his voice. The Lord reminded his people through Isaiah, "I did not speak in secret in a land of darkness. I the Lord speak with directness; I express myself with clarity" (Is 45:19). If we are not growing in union with the Lord employing techniques will be to no avail. But if we are genuinely seeking his face regularly in prayer, we are guaranteed to know what he wants of us. Put this together with a holy and wise spiritual director and you have the best formula for knowing the leading of the Spirit.

14

SPOUSE OF THE SPIRIT

My soul glorifies the Lord; my spirit rejoices in God, my Saviour. He looks on his servant in her lowliness; henceforth all ages will call me blessed (Lk 1:47-48).

Like all disciples of Jesus the Blessed Virgin Mary is a Temple of the Holy Spirit. However, she is more than this. Because of her unique role in the mystery of redemption she is often called "Spouse of the Spirit". Wherever Mary is, there will the Holy Spirit be present and evoked in the lives of others. She is radiant with the Spirit, totally transparent with the Spirit, completely docile to the Spirit. From the moment of her conception Mary was sanctified by the Holy Spirit. When the angel Gabriel appeared to her as a young woman in Nazareth, he greeted her as one "full of grace". But now she was to experience a new sending of the Spirit. When the angel announced she was to be the mother of the Messiah, she asked, "How can this be since I am a virgin." The angel replied, "The Holy Spirit will come upon you and the power of the Most High will overshadow you" (Lk 1:35). In the Old Testament, the *shekinah* cloud of glory overshadowed the Ark of the covenant. Now in the New Testament, the glory of God overshadowed the Virgin Mary. She had become the "Ark of the new covenant", no longer housing the commandments, but the eternal Son of God.

The Model Disciple

The Blessed Virgin Mary is woman of the Spirit, and hence our model of discipleship. Her faith, obedience and surrender to the Lord were expressed in her "fiat", "let it be done to me according to your will" (Lk 1:38). She shows us how to yield to the Spirit, and be docile to the Spirit's action. When she greets Elizabeth we are told "Elizabeth was filled with the Holy Spirit and exclaimed with a loud cry, 'Blessed are you among women, and blessed is the fruit of your womb, ... as soon as I heard the sound of your greeting, the child in my womb leaped for joy'" (Lk 1:44). Not only Elizabeth but also John the Baptist in his mother's womb was filled with the Spirit (see Lk 1:15). Mary's presence evoked the Holy Spirit in both of them. Then Mary bursts forth in a beautiful charismatic song of praise, "My soul glorifies the Lord, my spirit rejoices in God my saviour, because he has done great things for me. Holy is his name" (Lk 1:47). But she is also deeply contemplative in spirit. After the shepherds gave their news of great joy at the birth of Jesus, we are told Mary "treasured all these words and pondered them in her heart" (Lk 2:19).

Mary's journey of discipleship took her into ever deeper levels of surrender to God as she "learnt obedience through suffering" (Heb 5:8). Her initial "yes" to the angel, given with all her heart, had to be given again and again, and each time this meant a further expansion of her heart in response to the will of God. We think of the many crises she faced – the initial misunderstanding of Joseph, the mysterious words of Simeon that a sword would pierce her soul also, the terrifying flight into Egypt and the plight of being refugees in a foreign land, the loss of Jesus at the age of twelve with three days of frantic searching, then his enigmatic answer, "Did you not know I must be in my Father's house?" (Lk 2:49). We are told that when they returned to Nazareth after all the drama, "His mother treasured all these things in her heart" (Lk 2:51). No doubt she was somewhat perplexed by the unfolding of events, but each time she simply surrendered whole-heartedly to the will of God.

Then when the public ministry of Jesus began, his relatives thought he had gone crazy. How did she handle all of this? As opposition and enmity began to mount against him, how she must have suffered! They even tried to bustle him over a cliff just outside of Nazareth, but he eluded them. Again Mary was giving over all her consternation to the will of God. Then when he was arrested and put on trial, flogged, and carrying the heavy cross to Calvary, what she endured is difficult to imagine. The sword was piercing her soul. Yet she was to be found standing at the foot of the Cross, when grown men had run away in fear. Discipleship led by the Spirit takes us to the Cross. There her "yes" is consummated in loving obedience and surrender in union with the offering of her Son. The wounds in the hands and feet and side of Christ she experienced in her heart. If we ask the Blessed Virgin Mary she will take us with her to the foot of the Cross, and as we look upon the one whom we have pierced, we will know by the action of the Spirit the fire of love in the heart of Jesus for all men and women.

Mother of all Disciples

At the foot of the Cross in John's Gospel Mary is gathered with the small community of disciples. From the Cross Jesus turns to his Mother saying, "Woman, behold your son." And then to the Beloved disciple, "Behold your mother" (Jn 19:26-27). He gives Mary to us as Mother of all disciples, Mother of the Church. For John this is a symbolic moment of the Spirit being poured upon the Church, symbolized by the water flowing from the side of Christ. Just as Eve had been taken from the side of Adam, now the new Eve, the

Church, is born from the side of Christ. Mary is present in prayer at this moment of the releasing of the Spirit from the side of Christ, which birthed the Church.

In Luke's account of Pentecost we find Mary together with the apostles and many others in the upper room devoted to constant prayer believing with expectant faith in the promise of Jesus that they would experience an outpouring of the Holy Spirit (Acts 1:8,14). Already filled with the Spirit, Mary receives a new fullness of the Spirit at Pentecost as they were "all filled with the Holy Spirit and began to speak in other languages, as the Spirit gave them ability"(Acts 2:4). As Mother of the Church she is present with the other disciples to intercede for the Spirit's coming and as a member of the Church was baptized in the Spirit. She is a member of the Spirit-filled charismatic community of disciples. We can ask her to intercede for us and take us more deeply into the mystery of Pentecost, that we may know also the fire of the Spirit which enflames her soul. With the other disciples she was baptized in the Spirit and spoke in tongues and prophesied. She is the model charismatic disciple, just as she is the model contemplative disciple. These two dimensions of prayer are not in opposition to one another, but are found perfectly present and in harmony in the life of the Blessed Virgin Mary.

Maternal Intercession

Mary is our model for being alive in the Spirit, and by her intercession we receive an abundant outpouring of the Spirit. She teaches us how to pray both in a contemplative way as well as in charismatic praise, and she nurtures us in our life in the Spirit. Just as she taught Jesus from the Scriptures as he was growing up in Nazareth, so she teaches us also. Her presence protects us from evil and brings healing to our lives. She is the first evangelist; she was so filled with joy of the Christ within her, that her presence and her words released a quickening in Elizabeth's heart, and caused her child to leap in her womb. She is model of faith and obedience, and intercedes for us in time of spiritual battle.

We must be discerning about Marian devotion. If devotions to Mary are exercised in a way that chokes the working of the Spirit, then they should be purified. Our devotion is not primarily to Mary, but to Jesus and the Holy Spirit. Mary's whole desire is to see her Son glorified, not to draw attention to herself. At Cana in Galilee when the newly married couple were embarrassed because the wine had run out, she sized up the situation and went to Jesus, "They have no wine." Even though he hesitated to use his power, she simply said to the stewards, "Do whatever he tells you!" (Jn 2:5) This was the first time the glory of Jesus was manifest (Jn 2:11). In situations of life when we are desperate, when we have "run out of wine", we can turn to Mary, not to seek her power as such, but so that she may intercede for us. She is always ready to intercede on our behalf for the "new wine" of the Holy Spirit to be poured out in abundance. Our Marian devotion should release our spirit more fully into freedom, not chain us up in the bondage of law. Where Mary is genuinely present there will be the Holy Spirit, and where the Spirit is there is freedom. As Pope Paul VI wisely said, "Our primary devotion should be to the Holy Spirit to which devotion to the Blessed Virgin leads us, as it leads us to Christ."[97]

15
LAND OF THE SPIRIT

He changes desert into streams, thirsty ground into springs of water (Ps 107:35).

From the seventeenth century *Terra Australis* has been known by Europeans as "the Great South Land of the Holy Spirit". A Portugese explorer, Pedro Fernandez de Quiros, in search of the mysterious southern land thought he had found it when he anchored his ship on the coast of a small island off Vanuatu in May 1606. He ceremoniously proclaimed "I take possession of this part of the South as far as the pole in the name of Jesus ... which from now on shall be called the Southern Land of the Holy Spirit." The island where he landed is still called "Espiritu Santo". While Quiros never actually reached the Australian continent, the name he gave it still remains. Even though Quiros was mistaken about his location, he fully intended to dedicate the great southern continent to the Holy Spirit. While it would be overstating the significance of this event to claim it was "prophetic", nevertheless it was a providential sign. The name by which Australia came to be known, the *Great South Land of the Holy Spirit*, can inspire us to claim the promise that it brings. This country, which has the Southern Cross hanging in its skies, is meant to experience revival in the Holy Spirit.

The original Australians inhabited this Great South Land many centuries before Quiros made his journey. One of the descendants of these ancient people, Marjorie Liddy, a Tiwi woman from Melville island, was one of hundreds of indigenous children brought up in the missions, which multiplied across the Northern Territory from the mid-1930s. While it was a great sadness for the "stolen generation" to be taken from their families and land and put into mission schools, Marjorie has retained a deep love for the Church which brought her the faith, and she remains grateful for the mission. Marjorie's story of seeing a "big bird" in the sky in 2004 has now become part of Australian Catholic spiritual heritage. It is an indigenous sign of hope for the Australian Church. As Pope John Paul II said to the indigenous people at Alice Springs in 1986, "The Church in Australia will not be fully the Church that Jesus wants her to be until you have made your contribution to her life and until that contribution has been joyfully received by others."[98] Marjorie's story is best told from her own lips. On 30 August 2004 Marjorie was fishing with her son on the island:

> The moon was bright. But when we were walking back to the house, I noticed that it was suddenly really dark. I wondered, "what happened to the moon?" When I looked up, there was no moon, it had been covered by the shape of a bird all done in dots with wings that stretched out across the whole horizon. It had a beautiful golden halo at the top of its head. I asked my son if he saw what I could see. He said, "Yes mum, it's a bird". I said, "No son, that's the Holy Spirit. See the halo". And when I said that, a burst of golden sparkles started falling from the halo toward the earth. It was as if God's love was pouring out all over the land. My heart was filled with joy. While admiring its powerful wings, I started running toward the bird, trying to catch the golden sparkles and put them in my bag. When I was a little girl, I was taught a song about the Holy Spirit. I started dancing and singing this song too.

Wanting to capture what she had seen in the sky, Marjorie painted the image of the Holy Spirit depicted as the bird with a halo. Her painting was destined to become famous, since it was chosen as the icon for the World Youth Day celebrations in Sydney 2008, which had the theme, "You will receive power when the Holy Spirit comes upon you" (Acts 1:8). On the canopy over the stage where the Pope celebrated Mass the organizers attached an image of a huge bird painted in dots representing the Holy Spirit, just like Marjorie saw in the sky. "When I found out it had become a holy image, I cried," said Marjorie. "And when I saw it on the canopy over the Holy Father at World Youth Day, I just couldn't believe it." The image was also fashioned on the back of the specially designed chasubles worn by the priests during World Youth Day celebrations. "I have been so blessed by the Holy Spirit," says Marjorie. "I hope to continue spreading the story of God's love."

Marjorie is voicing the purpose of the Church – to spread the story of God's love. It is time for the Church in Australia to arise and fulfill its mission. Her image reminds us that God wants to pour out his Holy Spirit across this vast land with its diverse peoples like "golden sparkles" falling from the sky.

The number of people in Australia who call themselves Catholic is about 27% of the overall population. The Church is like a sleeping giant, waiting to be roused from slumber. Is this revival possible? How can it happen? I would suggest, only by the "kiss of the Spirit". Come Holy Spirit! If we were to rise up in our true identity, with the fire of the Holy Spirit upon us and within us, the impact upon the whole nation would be enormous.

So let us cry from the heart, *Veni Sancte Spiritus*, Come Holy Spirit, set your Church on fire again with zeal to preach in the name of Jesus. Make us one in you, so we can be a sign of love and unity to all peoples. Stir us from our lethargy, shake us out of our complacency, awaken us from our apathy.

Come Holy Spirit, bring springs in the desert; the life-giving waters of your Spirit to the hearts of our people. Come to this land of plenty to fill the emptiness of the hearts with your love. Pour out your love upon this thirsty land, melt our hearts, mould us in your image, fill us to overflowing, use us for your Kingdom. Come Holy Spirit fill the hearts of your faithful, enkindle in them the fire of your love. Send forth your Spirit and they shall be created and they shall renew the face of the earth.

ENDNOTES

[1] For a good overview of the experience see ICCRS Doctrinal Commission, *Baptism in the Spirit*, (Melbourne: CCR, 2012).

[2] I am thinking of the Catholic Fraternity of Covenant Communities and Fellowships which was inaugurated on 30 November 1990 as a Private Association of Christ's Faithful of Pontifical Right. It has a membership of around 40 communities from all continents.

[3] Because of the possibility of the term being misinterpreted to mean a second Baptism, some parts of the world prefer to use an alternative term, such as "effusion of the Spirit" or "release of the Spirit" or "outpouring of the Spirit". However, I prefer the term "baptism in the Spirit" since it retains the biblical language of John the Baptist and Jesus. See ICCRS Doctrinal Commission, *Baptism in the Spirit*, pp 60-61. Since I am using the baptismal language, the next chapter explains more fully the connection between the sacrament of Baptism and the "baptism in the Spirit".

[4] The last paragraph of this prayer is found in *Humanae Salutis*, the apostolic constitution by Pope John XXIII convoking the Council, dated 25 December 1961. Cf. Walter M. Abbott, General Editor, *The Documents of Vatican II* (New York: The American Press, 1966), pp 709, 793.

[5] Pope Paul VI, Apostolic Exhortation, *Gaudete in Domino* (On Christian Joy), 9 May 1975, 7.

[6] Pope John Paul II, Message at the meeting between Pope John Paul II and the ecclesial movements and new communities in St Peter's Square, Rome, 30 May 1998, in *Then Peter stood Up* (Rome: ICCRS, 2000) pp 91-93.

[7] Ibid., p 93.

[8] Pope Benedict XVI, "Let Baptism of the Holy Spirit purify every heart", 11 May 2008, *L'Ósservatore Romano*, English Edition, 14 May 2008, No. 20, 1.

[9] Pope John Paul II, *Address to the Charismatic Renewal*, 2002.

[10] Patti Gallagher Mansfield, *As By a New Pentecost* (Steubenville: Franciscan University Press, 1992) pp 39-40.

[11] Ibid., p 25.

[12] Christopher Ryan MGL, *In the Light of the Cross* (Strathfield: St Pauls Publications, 2009) pp 61-62.

[13] See an American analysis by Sherry A. Weddell, *Forming Intentional Disciples* (Huntington: Our Sunday Visitor, 2012) pp 28-37.

[14] See Raniero Cantalamessa, "Baptism in the Holy Spirit", *International Catholic Charismatic Renewal Services Newsletter* (online at http://catholiccharismatic.us/ccc/articles/cantalamessa, as of 8 May 2012). See also Raniero Cantalamessa, *Sober Intoxication of the Spirit* (Cincinatti: Servant Books, 2005) pp 38-53.

[15] Theology distinguishes between the action of God in the sacrament which is objectively accomplished (the "ex opera operato"), and the part that we play by our participation, depending on our freedom and disposition (the "ex opera operantis"). When a sacrament is valid the first is guaranteed to be present due to the will of Christ. However the fruitfulness of the sacrament in our lives depends on the disposition of the recipient. In Baptism the disposition needs to be faith, preceded by repentance.

[16] See a thorough study of this by Killian McDonnell and George T. Montague, *Christian Initiation and Baptism in the Holy Spirit: Evidence from the First Eight Centuries* (Collegeville: Liturgical Press, 1991) pp 83-349.

[17] Sherry Weddell, *Forming Intentional Disciples*, pp 64-70.

[18] See *Introduction to the Rite of Christian Initiation of Adults*, Par. 34.

[19] St Augustine, *On the Trinity*, VIII, 10, 14.

[20] See Fr Ken Barker, "Preaching: a Radical Call to Conversion", in *The New Evangelization* (Ballan: Connor Court, 2008) pp 53-69.

[21] Quoted in E. O'Connor, *Pope Paul and the Spirit* (Notre Dame, Ind: Ave Maria Press, 1978) p 183.

[22] For an exposition of the notion, see Raniero Cantalamessa, *A Sober Intoxication of the Spirit*, pp 1-19.

[23] John of the Cross, "The Living Flame of Love, Prologue 3-4", in *The Collected Works of St John of the Cross*, trans. Kieran Kavanaugh and Otilio Rodriguez (London: Thomas Nelson, 1966) p 578.

[24] Fr Augustine Vallooran, *Power from Above* (Challakudy, Kerala: Divine Retreat Centre, 2010).

[25] Basil the Great, *On the Holy Spirit*, IX, 22-23.

[26] Cyril of Jerusalem, *Catecheses*, XVI, 16.

[27] Raniero Cantalamessa, *Come Creator Spirit* (Collegeville, Minesota: Liturgical Press, 2003) pp 363-364.

[28] *Dei Verbum*, 12, in Vatican Council II, General Editor, Austin Flannery (Dublin: Dominican Publications, 1975) p 758.

[29] *Dei Verbum*, 21.

[30] See Fr Ken Barker, *Becoming Fire* (Balwyn: Freedom publishing, 2001) pp 22-23.

[31] Simeon, the New Theologian, *Catecheses*, IV.

[32] Basil, *On the Holy Spirit*, XIX, 49.

[33] Augustine, *Commentary on the Gospel of John*, 121, 4.

[34] Suggested by Raniero Cantalamessa, *Life in the Lordship of Christ* (London: Darton, Longman & Todd, 1992) p 128.

[35] John Cassian, *Conferences*, I, 18.

[36] Diadochus of Photike, *On Spiritual Knowledge*, in *The Philokalia* 1, (Boston: Faber and Faber, 1986) pp 259-60.

[37] Ibid.

[38] Cyprian of Carthage, *Ad Donatum*, 4, in *The Early Christian Fathers*, ed. Henry Bettenson (Oxford: Oxford University Press, 1956).

[39] See 1 Cor 12:4-11; 1 Cor 12:27-28; Rom 12:3-8 ; Eph 4:11-13.

[40] J.D.G. Dunn, *Jesus and the Spirit* (London: SCM Press, 1975) p 255.

[41] This section and the following section on the history has been strongly influenced by Raniero Cantalamessa, *Come Creator Spirit*, pp 175-184.

[42] See Frederick L. Moriarty SJ, "Isaiah 1-39", in *The Jerome Biblical Commentary*, ed. Brown, Fitzmyer and Murphy (London: Geoffrey Chapman, 1968) p 273.

[43] See Ronald A. Knox, *Enthusiasm* (Westminster: Christian Classics, 1950) pp 25-49.

[44] Irenaeus, *Against the Heresies*, V, 6, 1.

[45] *Lumen Gentium*, 12, in *Vatican Council II*, General Editor Austin Flannery (Dublin: Dominican Publications, 1975) p 363.

[46] I am indebted in this section to Sr Nancy Kellar, "the Gifts of the Spirit", *ICCRS Newsletter*, Vol.IV, no.6 (November-December 1998) pp 1-2. The reader is recommended to explore discerning the gifts using Sherry Weddell, *The Catholic Spiritual Gifts Inventory*, from The Catherine of Siena Institute, Seattle Washington.

[47] See the principles outlined by Pope Paul VI, Address to the Catholic

Charismatic Renewal at Second International Leaders Conference, Rome, 19 May 1975, in *Then Peter Stood Up*, pp 19-21.

48 For an expansive description of these virtues, see Fr Ken Barker, *Becoming Fire* (Balwyn: Freedom publishing, 2001) pp 52-72.

49 See Pope John Paul II, Message at the meeting between Pope John Paul II and the ecclesial movements and new communities in St Peter's Square, Rome, 30 May 1998, in *Then Peter Stood Up*, p 89.

50 This phrase was first used by Pope Paul VI, Address to the Catholic Charismatic Renewal at Second International Leaders Conference, Rome, 19 May 1975, in *Then Peter Stood Up*, p 17.

51 Image used by Raniero Cantalamessa, *Come Creator Spirit*, p 188.

52 Thérèse of Liseux, *Story of a Soul*, trans. John Clarke OCD (Washington: ICS Publications, 1976) p 194.

53 Congregation for Doctrine and Faith, *Instruction on Prayers for Healing*, Section 2. Par. 1.

54 Francis Martin, *The Life-Changer* (Ann Arbor Michigan, Servant Publications, 1990) p 135.

55 Dante Alighieri, *Paridiso Canto*, III, 85.

56 St Augustine, *Confessions*, XXII, 9.

57 Basil the Great, *On the Holy Spirit*, XIX, 49.

58 For a fuller presentation of temptation, see Fr Ken Barker, *Becoming Fire*, pp 36-43. In this discussion of evil I am indebted to *Manual of Minor Exorcisms*, compiled by Bishop Julian Porteous (London: Catholic Truth Society, 2012) pp 6-21.

59 These three characteristics are from Ignatius Loyola, *Rules for the Discernment of Spirits*, 325-327.

60 Pope John Paul II, Wednesday Audience, 1983.

61 The details of this testimony are taken from http://www.ccr.org.uk/testimony/trapped.htm. See also David Payne, *Alive* (Cafe Resources, 2009).

62 St Augustine, *Exposition on the Psalms*, 143,7.

63 See *The Rite of Christian Initiation for Adults*, 156.

64 Cyril of Jerusalem, *Catecheses*, XVI, 19.

65 *Catechism of the Catholic Church*, 2560.

[66] George T. Montague, "Riding the Spirit", in *The Spirit and the Church*, compiled by Ralph Martin (New York: Paulist Press, 1976) pp 172-173.

[67] St Augustine, *Commentary on Psalm 32*, II, 8.

[68] Ibid.

[69] Quoted in Paul Hinnebush OP, *Praise: A Way of Life* (Ann Arbor: Servant Books, 1976) pp 47-48.

[70] John Cassian, *Conferences*, 10, 11 p 138.

[71] *Catechism of the Catholic Church*, 2672.

[72] Pope Paul VI, *Evangelii Nuntiandi*, 75.

[73] Sermons of St Anthony of Padua, 1, 226. See in Office of Readings, June 13.

[74] This section on anointing has been inspired by Raniero Cantalamessa, *The Holy Spirit in the Life of Jesus* (Collegeville: Liturgical Press, 1994) pp 5-18. See also the same author, *The Creator Spirit*, pp 151-170.

[75] See Fr Ken Barker, "Preaching: a Radical Call to Conversion", in *The New Evangelization*, ed. Bishop Julian Porteous, pp 53-61.

[76] Pope Paul VI, *Evangelii Nuntiandi*, 18.

[77] Pope John Paul II, *Redemptoris Missio*, 46.

[78] Pope John Paul II, *Christifideles Laici*, 33.

[79] Pope Paul VI, *Evangelii Nuntiandi*, 14.

[80] Pope John Paul II, *Redemptoris Missio*, 90.

[81] Pope John Paul II, *Redemptoris Missio*, 3.

[82] Pope John Paul II, *Redemptoris Missio*, 42.

[83] Pope Paul VI, *Evangelii Nuntiandi*, 27.

[84] Pope John Paul II, *Redemptoris Missio*, 46.

[85] Pope Paul VI, *Evangelii Nuntiandi*, 24.

[86] Pope John Paul II, "The Task of the Latin American Bishop", *Origins* 12 (24 March 1983), 659-62.

[87] Pope John Paul II, "Address to Bishops of Latin America", *L'Osservatore Romano*, English Language Edition, 21 October 1992.

[88] John Paul II, *Redemptoris Missio*, 33.

[89] John Paul II, *Novo Millenio Ineunte*, 40.

[90] John Cassian, *Conferences*, 1, 20, trans. Colm Luibheid (New Jersey: Paulist Press, 1985) p 54.

[91] The story is adapted from Thomas H. Green SJ, *Weeds Among the Wheat* (Notre Dame Indiana: Ave Maria Press, 1984) p 61.

[92] This is a practice from Ignatitus Loyola's *Spiritual Exercises*, which was presented in a contemporary way by George A. Aschenbrenner, SJ, "Consciousness Examen", *Review for Religious*, Vol. 31 (1972:1): pp 14-21. Presented in brief form in Fr Ken Barker, *Becoming Fire* (Balwyn: Freedom Publishing, 2001) pp 167-168.

[93] John Henry Newman, *Meditations and Devotions*, Part III (1848).

[94] We find this in his *Spiritual Exercises*. A good popular presentation is found in Timothy M. Gallagher, *Discerning the Will of God* (New York: Crossroads, 2009).

[95] Ignatius Loyola, *The Spiritual Exercises*, 316, 3, trans. Louis J. Puhl SJ (Chicago: Loyola University Press, 1951) p 142.

[96] Ignatius Loyola, *The Spiritual Exercises*, 317, 4, op. cit., p 142.

[97] Paul VI, quoted in Edward O'Connor, *Pope Paul and the Spirit* (Notre Dame: Ave Maria Press, 1978) p 184.

[98] Pope John Paul II, "Address to Aboriginal and Torres Strait Islander Peoples", November 1986, par 13 in *The Pope in Australia* (Homebush: St Pauls Publications, 1986), p 172.

www.ingramcontent.com/pod-product-compliance
Lightning Source LLC
Chambersburg PA
CBHW032252150426
43195CB00008BA/426